There's no better doctor
than a good cook

(German proverb)

Kannenbäckerland is the name given to an area in the Westerwald in Germany, roughly between Coblenz and Limburg. The name means "Potter's Country" and is certainly very apposite, for the region has been famous for the production of ceramics for generations. Its pretty vases and drinking-mugs are especially well-known. Ransbach, the home of Eduard Bay, is in the heart of this country, and the RÖMERTOPF is a product typical of the tradition both in type and quality.

First-class products are bound to be imitated, so when buying your porous earthenware casserole, watch for the following points :

● handy shape, easily removed lid ;

● even finish on the inside, without any rims which would make cleaning difficult ;

● ridges on the bottom inside, which ensure even browning and prevent the food from sticking ;

● the guarantee of quality from an institute of domestic science ;

● the name RÖMERTOPF on the lid.

The Bay-RÖMERTOPF fulfils all these requirements.

The authoress about herself:

After having studied modern languages in England, I came to Germany five years ago to teach English at the University of Munich. Although I had for several years been keenly interested in international cookery it never occurred to me at that time that I would myself write a cookery book. In Munich, however, I soon had a circle of friends whose gastronomical interests were not just a hobby, but also part of their professions. We were soon exchanging and testing national recipes and personal ideas on food. During the course of my five years here this exchange has increased and included collection of ideas on cooking during trips throughout Germany, and in other parts of Europe. The idea of adapting the German RÖMERTOPF cookery book was thus for me from the very start a fascinating one. The actual collecting, comparing and trying out of the recipes included in the book has been equally satisfying. The hobby has not supplanted the teaching in any way — but has certainly provided a pleasing addition and contrast to the spheres of German-English interest with which I am normally occupied.

Wendy Philipson

WENDY PHILIPSON

RÖMERTOPF®

cooking is fun

Over 350 delicious recipes for
healthy, tasty, easily-prepared food.

For all lovers of good cooking
from the sole manufacturers of the RÖMERTOPF
EDUARD BAY, D-5412, RANSBACH-W-GERMANY

English adaptation
completely reworked and extended by Wendy Philipson,
from the original German "Braten und Schmoren im
RÖMERTOPF"

If you would like more information about
the RÖMERTOPF please write to

RÖMERTOPF-Service USA:

RECO International Corp.
P.O. Box 591
Port Washington, N.Y. 11050
Tel. 516/767-2400

RÖMERTOPF - international

D-5412 Ransbach/W. Germany
tel : (02623) 2048

10 th English edition.
420-470 thousand.
© by Eduard BAY, Ransbach, 1971
Printed in Belgium by Scorpion s.a., Verviers.
Cover design : Atelier Heinrichs & Bachmann, Munich.
ISBN : 3-87059-087-4.
BAY-Order no. : 980 87

CONTENTS

Advantages of RÖMERTOPF Cooking

No doubt many of the readers of this little book will already be well acquainted with RÖMERTOPF cooking ; to others, however, it may be an entirely new and unknown method of preparing food. Therefore, before going on to discuss recipes, and make suggestions for actual cooking, we would like to tell you why we think that it is such an excellent method of cooking. The RÖMERTOPF easily meets three main criteria we set for good cooking methods : food prepared in it tastes excellent ; it is very healthy ; and the actual preparation of the food is simple and pleasant. Cookery is an art, but it should also be fun. With a RÖMERTOPF we think it is — both for cook and eater !

The RÖMERTOPF is, of course, not really a new discovery — it is a rediscovery. With the RÖMERTOPF a method of cooking has been rediscovered which dates back over thousands of years. The Romans, well-known not only for their military conquests, their law and architecture, but also as lovers of pleasure, of good wines and food, used this method to produce really excellent meals. They cooked in earthenware casseroles. And even before them, our most primitive ancestors, who lived from the fruits of the hunt, cooked the meat of the animals they had killed in simple clay containers placed in the glowing embers of their fires. Both these methods were basically the same. And they were not merely used because no other method of cooking food had been discovered then. On the contrary. Lucullus, the first true gourmet, was well acquainted with metal cooking pans, but he nevertheless prefered — as do modern gourmets — to use earthenware dishes. Why ?

For several reasons

It is possible to cook food in an earthenware casserole with a minimum of liquid, or even without adding any liquid at all. This means that the natural juices, the full flavour and taste, the essential nutrients and vitamins, are all retained intact and not simply thrown away with the excess liquid. The aroma and taste of food prepared in this way is rich and nutritious. The food is therefore not impaired in any way during the cooking process and its taste is really excellent.

It is also possible to cook almost all kinds of food without the addition of any fat — thus fulfilling the strict requirements of modern dietetics (and of prime importance for those on a diet either for health reasons, or because they desire to slim). This has been officially verified by the Institute of Domestic Science in Munich — and the Bay-RÖMERTOPF is the only casserole of its kind which has been subjected to these tests. Food cooked in the RÖMERTOPF is thus excellent by health standards. The German Diabetics Association, for example, uses the Bay-RÖMERTOPF in its courses on cooking and nutrition. If you suffer from any disturbances of the stomach or liver, if you want to slim or stay slim, or if you are just a normally healthy person who attaches some importance to staying normally healthy, then you will find this method of cooking ideal for you. As you will see, many of our recipes do include fat — added to improve the taste — but in almost all of them the fat ingredients may be left out, if desired.

And, what is more, cooking in a RÖMERTOPF is really child's play. "Overdone" and "burnt" are words which are completely unknown in the RÖMERTOPF kitchen. Once a dish is in the oven nothing can go wrong. The cook does not need to bother about it again, until her family, or her guests, are waiting to be served — she's on holiday, so to speak (from food preparation at least !) whilst the food is cooking itself. This is, of course, an immense advantage both to mothers with young families, who thus have more time for their children, and for busy hostesses — what is more impressive than being able to turn out a first-class meal to guests without appearing to have taken any trouble at all !

Apart from these three major advantages the RÖMERTOPF is excellent in many other, perhaps unexpected, ways. It is attractive as well as useful. Nowadays, with modern technical developments, not only in outer space but also in the kitchen, the housewife is grateful for every technical improvement — from the high-speed pressure cooker to the fully automatic oven. Yet sometimes we think wistfully that with all this progress the cosiness of the old-fashioned kitchen is being lost. The RÖMERTOPF — much to our delight — combines the best of both worlds : it has technical perfection (and, as we all know, all really perfect things are in essence very simple) and yet retains something of the atmosphere of those homely old kitchens which were full of marvellous smells and beautiful cooking utensils. It is quite attractive enough, too, to be brought straight from the oven to the dining table (practical again — this saves washing up !).

In the course of your "acquaintance" with the Bay-RÖMERTOPF you will be ever more delighted by " minor " advantages. Its shape, for example. In contrast to other models on the market the Bay-RÖMERTOPF has a practical wide bottom which ensures a firm stand and thus avoids its being accidentally tipped over and causing nasty scalds. It has a broad lip in the middle to ensure that base and cover fit well. Between the base and the cover, by the way, you will notice that there is a small gap of about an eighth of an inch. Don't think that this is a fault — it is a means of regulating pressure — by allowing excess steam to escape. The handles have also been carefully designed so that the pot is easily lifted and very handy to use. One final, very important, point : the ridges on the bottom. The corrugated bed of the RÖMERTOPF ensures that the meat, fish or vegetables being cooked in it are lifted out of the juices and can thus brown on all sides evenly (this corrugated bed is an invention of the firm of Eduard Bay).

There are, of course, several models to choose from (and you may well soon decide that you want a second one for sweets, for fish, or to give to someone else as a present). The RÖMERTOPF comes in two colours — natural beige and warm red. Which colour you select is entirely a matter of personal taste, for there is absolutely no difference in quality. As well as the small and family-sized casseroles, there is also an extra large one (big enough to accommodate the Christmas turkey) and a longer, shallower dish specially for fish. Each of the dishes bears an appropriate design on its lid.

How to Use Your RÖMERTOPF

The RÖMERTOPF is not a gadget which is very complicated to use, but there are nonetheless a few basic " rules " which should be borne in mind when using it. It will certainly render you good service — if you look after it properly.

The most important thing is that every time you want to use the casserole you should first soak it in water for 15 minutes. There is a very good reason for this. The Roman Pot is made of special porous material and is unglazed so that it can " breathe " during the entire cooking process. The pores are filled with water before cooking by soaking so that a slight moist haze forms within the casserole. The food thus cooks in a completely natural way ; it is cooked right through without drying out at all. If the lid of the casserole is removed for the final ten minutes of the cooking process an especially crisp finish is obtained. This means that meat is tender, juicy and crisp ; that all the ingredients of a stew are delightfully and perfectly combined ; and that soups can cook slowly without losing any of their moisture. Once you have grown accustomed to putting the casserole into water, it presents no problem. When you first start to prepare a meal place the dish in cold water in the sink — by the time you have collected and prepared the necessary ingredients, the dish is ready to go into the oven. Since it is perhaps easy, at the beginning, to forget this soaking, we have referred to it in every recipe. The first time you use the casserole it is a good idea to soak it longer — for about half an hour — and to brush it out thoroughly, to make sure that all the dust is completely removed.

Cleaning your RÖMERTOPF presents no problem at all. All you need is hot water and a washing-up brush or the special RÖMER-

TOPF-cleaner. A few drops of washing-up liquid in the water make the cleaning easier and will not harm the casserole in any way. But *never* brush out the dish with Ajax or Vim or similar scourers! This will only result in the pores becoming blocked and will ruin the natural cooking process. After you have used the Roman Pot a few times it will become a little discoloured — especially if it is a beige one. But this is not at all important. You *know* that you have brushed away all the remains of food and that the dish is perfectly clean. Do not let these slight stains tempt you into scouring the pot. After you have used it about a hundred times you can treat it to a special "spring-clean". Boil it out for about half an hour so that the pores are completely cleaned out and the pot can breathe again. When the dish is not in use it is best kept in an airy place. Don't close it in the way you do for cooking, but place the lid upside down on top of the base to allow the air to circulate freely.

The RÖMERTOPF is only for use in the oven. Never stand it on a hot cooking plate or over an open flame!

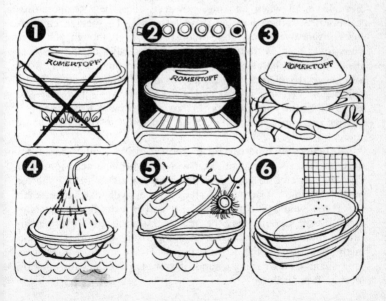

The RÖMERTOPF does not like sudden and violent changes in temperature. When you take it out of the hot oven, it is safest to place it on a folded dish-cloth or tea towel rather than placing it on a very cold metal or stone surface. Similarly, once the RÖMERTOPF has been put into the oven, and has become hot, you should not add any *cold* liquids. If more liquid has to be added during the cooking process, it should always be warmed a little first.

To sum up:
● Never use over an open flame.
● Into the oven. The oven stays clean.
● When you take it out of a hot oven, stand it on a cloth.
● Soak before using.
● Clean with hot water and a washing-up brush.
● Store in an airy place, with the lid resting upside down inside the base.

The RÖMERTOPF is equally well suited for use in electric and gas ovens. We have given settings for both in all our recipes. Bear in mind when cooking, however, that these temperatures are pointers rather than hard and fast rules. The actual temperatures inside ovens vary tremendously and even though you have your oven set at the temperature stated the degree of heat inside may not be at all the same as that in our test oven. After you have tried out the casserole a few times you will be completely at home with it and will know how — if at all — to vary the given temperatures. In any case, in the RÖMERTOPF, a change in temperature will certainly not result in your food being ruined.

The length of time needed to cook a dish will also vary from oven to oven — but again, you will soon become accustomed to this. Be prepared to cook food for a longer rather than a shorter period of time. Steamed and stewed foods will take longer than those you would like to have crisp and brown. For a specially crisp finish, the lid may be removed during the final ten to fifteen minutes cooking time. In comparison with other cooking methods a dish in the RÖMERTOPF will take up to a quarter as long again — bear this in mind, if you adapt recipes for cooking in your Roman Pot.

Always put the RÖMERTOPF **into a cold oven. With an electric oven you can then set the required temperature and the oven will heat up gradually and naturally. Select the oven setting which gives even heating from above and below. Gas ovens should be heated slowly. It is best first to set a low regulo number and to increase this every five minutes until you have set the required number.**

It only remains to wish you happy cooking. The recipes in this book are a selection from all over the world. Some may be old favourites, specially adapted for preparation in the RÖMER- TOPF ; others will be completely new to you. We hope that you enjoy trying them out — and that you find many more of your own. Once you have grown accustomed to cooking in your Roman Pot you can go ahead and invent your own superb dishes. Experimenting is always exciting — and with the Roman Pot there is less danger of failure than with many cooking methods. So go ahead and good luck — RÖMERTOPF cooking is fun !

Measures

The measures given in the recipes are according to the American standard. This means that the British housewife must make slight alterations when measuring out ingredients given in cups or pints. An American cup and the American pint are smaller than the English. Anyone accustomed to following the British standard should therefore use a little less (cf. British measures) of such ingredients than he normally would — or, alternatively, increase the amount of the other ingredients. The following table is provided as a guide.

	American	*British* *(and Canadian)*
Liquid measure	1 pint (= 16 fluid oz.)	⅘ pint
	1 cup (= 8 fluid oz.)	⅖ pint
	1 ¼ pint	1 pint (= 20 fluid oz.)

Solid measure

butter	2 cups	1 lb.
flour	4 cups	1 lb.
sugar	2 cups	1 lb.
rice	2 cups	1 lb.
dried fruit (average)	2 cups	1 lb.
minced meat	2 cups	1 lb.

Ingredients measured in pounds and ounces, and other measures used, are the same in both standards.

The recipes will give four good helpings, unless otherwise stated.

Abbreviations

tbs.	tablespoon
tsp.	teaspoon
oz.	ounce
lb.	pound

For easy and convenient cleaning of your „Römertopf"
The pot with dried in frying residues is soaked for 5-10 minutes in hot water with a few drops of cleansing agent.

With the rough side of the „kliner" the frying residues are scraped out. This will remove all the dirt.

With the fine side of the „kliner" the pot is again wiped out, after it has been carefully rinsed.
The pot is then left to dry in an airy place.

MEAT RECIPES

Cooking a joint in the RÖMERTOPF is really simple : just put the meat in the casserole, pop it in the oven and forget about it for about 2 hours ! Then it's ready. It's a good idea to add a little additional liquid (but not essential) in the case of veal and beef in particular, to guarantee that the meat does not become too dry. When the meat is cooked, take it out of the casserole and put it to keep warm. Then carefully remove the juice from the bottom of the dish and pour it into a saucepan. If required add a little stock or water to increase amount. Then simply thicken with flour and you have a perfect gravy — which you can make even more delicious, by adding a little wine or sour cream. Now you have a perfect roast and a mouth-watering sauce to serve with it.

The RÖMERTOPF is equally good for preparing dishes of sliced and diced meat. Goulash and similar dishes can be prepared with the addition of only a minimum of liquid without any danger of the meat being caught — and the gravy at the end is full of the natural juices and flavour of the meat.

Beef

With beef, more than with any other kind of meat, the quality of the meat you buy is of major importance. Or course, the slow RÖMERTOPF method of cooking is ideal for tougher cuts that require slower cooking, as well as for younger, tender meat — but even a RÖMERTOPF can't make poor quality, flabby old beef taste like fresh young meat. So don't blame the RÖMERTOPF unjustifiably if the meat you have bought is old and tough !

Make sure that your meat is well hung if not leave it to stand for some time covered with oil, then wipe it well before cooking. Remember that our principle of being prepared to lengthen the cooking period rather than shorten it is of prime importance with beef.

Very lean beef ought to be basted from time to time during cooking to prevent it drying out — it does not have much fat or juice of its own.

Here are a few recipe suggestions :

Roman Pot Beef

These quantities will give up to six helpings :
● *2 lb. braising beef*   *1 onion*
   2-3 mixed vegetables   *1 tbs. mixed herbs*
   salt and pepper

Place the cleaned joint in the soaked RÖMERTOPF, arrange the sliced vegetables around it and sprinkle with salt and pepper. Cover and cook in a hot oven (400 F. - Gas mark 6) until tender — this will depend upon the meat, but should take about 2½ hours. If you would like a nice crispy brown joint remove the lid of the casserole during the last ten minutes cooking time. The liquid can then be poured off and thickened in a saucepan to make an excellent gravy.

If you want to give a special touch to the joint and surprise the family, pour half a cup of red wine over it before cooking. The wine will flavour the meat and really enhance the taste of the gravy.

● There are many **national variations** to this basic recipe. Here are a few :
○ *The French* like to brown the joint in a little hot butter in a frying pan before putting it into the braising pot. Then they cook it with 5-6 small, peeled onions, a bay leaf and a little thyme — and, of course, a glass of wine. They sprinkle the joint generously with chopped parsley before serving.

○ *In Bohemia* the meat is covered with sliced bacon before cooking and the final fifteen minutes is done without the lid of the casserole, so that the bacon becomes crispy brown.

○ *In Hungary* they add a few spoonfuls of sour cream, two chopped anchovies, two chopped sweet peppers, 1 tbs. lemon juice, a little grated lemon rind, 1 tbs. capers and a little crushed garlic.

Try out some of these variations — then make up some of your own !

Rolled Beef Slices

● *4 large, thin slices of*
  beef
  2 tbs. oil
  ½ tsp. capers
  ½ glass red wine
  salt and pepper

2 tbs. mustard
2 tbs. chopped bacon
2 onions
1 tsp. chopped herbs
½ pint stock
1 tsp. flour

Brush the beef with oil and leave for at least 2 hours. Then remove the excess oil and rub with salt and pepper. Spread mustard on one side. Then add the capers, 1 chopped onion and the chopped bacon. Spread evenly on the slices. Then roll up the meat and tie with string or pierce with a skewer. The meat may then be quickly browned in the frying pan. Transfer to the soaked RÖMERTOPF and sprinkle on the remaining chopped onion. Pour on the wine. Cover and cook in a hot oven (400 F. - Gas mark 6) for 1½ hours. Whilst the meat is cooking mix ½ pint stock with the flour. Then take the RÖMERTOPF out of the oven and stir the stock into the liquid in the pot. Put the pot back into the oven for a further ten minutes to allow the meat to brown.

The meat slices may also be filled with a mixture of minced meat, a little chopped bacon and onion, pinch of salt, some chopped parsley and grated lemon rind.

Or fill the meat with pieces of cheese, or chopped hard-boiled egg.

Slimming : these rolled beef slices are not fattening in themselves, but are highly spiced and cannot therefore be eaten on
their own. The potatoes or rice served with them make them
unsuitable for anyone watching his waist line !

Sliced Beef with Mushrooms

● *1 lb. sirloin* *½ lb. mushrooms*
  1 onion *1 tbs. butter*
  1 tsp. mustard *1 cup stock*
  1 tbs. flour *1 tbs. lemon juice*
  1 cup red wine *salt and pepper*

Cut the meat into thin slices, season with salt and pepper. Chop
the onion and fry the meat and onion in hot butter until
browned. Then transfer to the soaked RÖMERTOPF. Mix together
the stock, red wine, mustard, lemon juice and flour. Add the
mushrooms to the meat, then pour over the liquid. Cover and
cook for about 45 minutes in a medium oven (375 F. - Gas
mark 5). Season to taste.
   Serve with boiled potatoes and cauliflower.

Sliced beef prepared like this is not suitable for slimmers !

Goulash

● *1 lb. beef (or pork -* *2 onions*
     or mix both) *1 oz. dripping*
  1 sweet pepper *2 tsp. paprika pepper*
  2 tbs. flour *a little grated lemon*
  1 cup stock *rind*
  salt

Chop the onions, dice the meat and fry together in hot dripping
in a frying pan. (This stage may be omitted, if you wish to make
preparation of the dish simpler, but it gives the meat a brown
finish and seals in the juices at the start). Then transfer to the

soaked RÖMERTOPF. Remove the seeds from the pepper, chop and sprinkle this on top of the meat and onions. Add the stock and flavour with salt, paprika pepper (plenty !) and grated lemon rind. Cover and cook in a moderate oven (375 F. - Gas mark 5) for about 2½ hours. Before serving add flour to thicken and further seasonings to taste.

Serve with boiled potatoes or rice.

● There are lots of **variations** for goulash ; here are a few :
- use red wine instead of stock ;
- add two crushed cloves of garlic ;
- flavour with caraway seeds ;
- add finely chopped gherkins just before the end of the cooking time ;
- omit the sweet pepper and in its place add a small tin of mushrooms half an hour before the end of the cooking time ;
- add tomato puree to the stock ;
- pour on wine or sour cream before serving ;
- add two small, sliced sausages just before the cooking is finished.

The most famous goulash of all comes from Szeged in Hungary. To make genuine *Szegediner Goulash* you should add 1 tbs. caraway seeds and 1 lb. sauerkraut at the beginning..

Hungarian Shepherd's Goulash

● *1 lb. meat (mixed)*   *½ lb. onions*
  ½ lb. tomatoes   *½ lb. sweet peppers.*
  2 tbs. butter   *paprika pepper*
  salt

Chop the onions and cut the butter into small pieces. Put these together into the bottom of the soaked RÖMERTOPF, then add the cored and sliced peppers, the diced meat, salt and plenty of paprika pepper. Cover and cook in a hot oven (400 F. - Gas mark 6) for about two hours.

● Just two **variations** to this :
- add ½ lb. sauerkraut at the beginning ;
- add chopped raw potatoes and 1 cup water.

Beef Ragout with Burgundy

These quantities will give six good helpings :

● *2½ lb. beef (off bone)*   *1½ cups burgundy*
  12 oz. mushrooms   *1 sweet pepper*
  2 onions   *1 bay leaf*
  1 clove garlic   *2 tbs. butter*

Dice the meat and marinade overnight in the wine. On the following day drain off the wine. Sauté the sliced mushrooms and chopped onions in hot butter, add the meat and let it brown a little. Then transfer all to the soaked RÖMERTOPF and add the sliced pepper, crushed garlic, bay leaf plus salt and pepper to taste. Pour over one cup of the wine. Cover and cook in a hot oven (400 F. - Gas mark 6) for 2½ hours — or until meat is tender.

Serve with boiled noodles with butter and fresh salad.

Minced Beef

● *1 lb. minced beef*   *2 cups boiled macaroni*
  1 tin mushrooms   *(not soft)*
  2 onions   *2 small tins tomato*
  1 clove of garlic   *puree*
  ½ cup red wine   *salt and pepper*

Slice the mushrooms, chop the onions and mix these with the meat. Place the boiled macaroni in the bottom of the soaked RÖMERTOPF and cover with the meat. Sprinkle with salt and pepper and add the crushed garlic. Stir the tomato puree into the wine and pour this over the meat. Cover and cook in a hot oven (400 F. - Gas mark 6) for just over an hour.

● As a variation :
- sprinkle the finished dish generously with grated cheese and return to the oven without the lid to allow to brown.

Sauerbraten
(beef steeped in vinegar and then roasted)

● *1½ lb. beef*
2 tbs. cornflour
2 gherkins
salt and pepper
mixed herbs

For the marinade :

½ pint vinegar
1 bay leaf
2 cloves
2 peppercorns
1 onion, sliced

The meat should be first well beaten and steeped in the marinade at least overnight. Remove from the marinade, dry and rub with salt and pepper. Put into the soaked RÖMERTOPF and sprinkle with chopped herbs. Pour on a little of the marinade — about 1 inch deep in the pot. Cover and cook in a hot oven (400 F. - Gas mark 6) for about 2 ½ hours. Remove the cover of the pot during the last 20 minutes to allow the meat to brown. Then drain off the liquid, strain through a sieve and thicken with the cornflour. Add the chopped gherkins to this gravy.

Serve with dumplings, boiled potatoes or rice.

The meat can, as an alternative, be larded after being removed from the marinade — or place a few slices of bacon in the pot underneath the joint.

One variation which is very popular in Scandinavia and Northern Germany is adding slices of apple which have been gently steamed for a short time.

An alternative marinade can simply be buttermilk or sour milk.

Diet : for the same reasons as stuffed beef rolls — i.e., that it is rather highly spiced and therefore cannot be eaten on its own — sauerbraten is not really suitable.

Shepherd's Pie

- *1 lb. minced meat*   *1-2 onions*
  chopped herbs   *small cup stock*
  salt and pepper   *chopped herbs*
  1 ½ lb. mashed potatoes

Chop and heat the onion in a frying pan. Add the meat and allow to brown a little. Then transfer to the soaked RÖMERTOPF, add the salt and herbs and pour on the stock. Cover and cook in a hot oven (450 F. - Gas mark 8) for about 30 minutes (until the meat is cooked through). Remove from the oven and cover the meat with the mashed potatoes ; spread out evenly. Then return to the oven and cook until the potatoes are nicely golden brown on top — alternatively you could pop the dish under the grill for a few minutes.

The dish can be improved by adding ¼-½ lb. chopped mushrooms to the meat at the beginning.

Stewed Ox-tail

- *1 ox-tail, jointed*   *1 onion*
  2oz. dripping   *1 carrot*
  ½ pint stock   *½ pint red wine*
  2 tbs. wine vinegar   *2 cloves*
  bouquet garni   *1 bay leaf*
  salt and pepper   *1 clove of garlic*
  lemon rind

Put the vinegar in a saucepan, add the seasonings and bring quickly to the boil. Marinade the ox-tail in this overnight. Place the ox-tail with a cup of the marinade in the soaked RÖMERTOPF. Melt the dripping in a saucepan, stir in the flour and heat until it turns yellow. Add the stock and stir well until it thickens. Pour onto the other ingredients in the RÖMERTOPF and add the bouquet garni. Cover and cook for 3-4 hours in a hot oven (400 F. - Gas mark 6).

Tastes excellent served with boiled potatoes and a green vegetable. But for a change try boiled noodles with a little melted butter.

The stew can be varied by adding a few chopped mushrooms.

Curried Beef

- 2 lb. beef (off bone)   1 tbs. dessicated coconut
  2 tbs. sultanas   1 large baking apple
  1 tomato   1 onion
  6 tbs. flour   2 tbs. curry powder
  1 cup stock   salt and pepper
  1 tsp. brown sugar

Cut the meat into cubes ; peel and chop the vegetables. Then fry the meat and vegetables in a little hot fat. Transfer to the soaked RÖMERTOPF. Add the stock, sultanas, sugar, salt, curry powder, coconut. Cover and cook in a medium oven (375 F. - Gas mark 5) for about 2 hours. Thicken with flour.

Serve with boiled rice and lime pickle or mango chutney.

Veal

When cooking veal it is a good idea always to add about 1 cup of liquid — because there is hardly any fat in the meat and it would otherwise dry out. Apart from that there are no special rules about cooking veal.

Roman Pot Veal

- 3 lb. veal (off bone)   a few chopped mushrooms
  1 onion   1 carrot
  ¼ pint stock   ½ pint sour cream
  salt and pepper

Beat and wash the meat. Rub with salt and pepper. Put a few small pieces of butter into the soaked RÖMERTOPF. Then add the meat and pour the stock over it. Scatter the chopped vegetables on top and cover. Cook in a hot oven (400 F. - Gas mark 6) for about 2½ hours. The cover may be removed during the final ten minutes to allow the meat to brown. Then drain off the liquid and put the meat to keep warm. Heat the liquid with the sour cream in a saucepan. Season to taste. If the gravy is not thick enough a little flour may be added.

Serve with boiled potatoes and green vegetables.

If you like to have your veal really brown and crispy then brush it with a mixture of beaten egg and breadcrumbs before putting it into the oven.

Knuckle of Veal

● *1 knuckle of veal*　　　*½ cup white wine*
　½ cup sour cream　　　*1 tbs. butter*
　paprika pepper　　　　*salt and pepper*

Wash the knuckle, rub in salt and pepper and sprinkle with a little paprika pepper. Brush on a little melted butter and put in the soaked RÖMERTOPF. Cover and cook in a hot oven (400 F. - Gas mark 6) until tender — this will take about 2½ hours. Baste about once an hour. Then drain off the liquid and replace the meat in the oven — without the cover — to brown (or pop it under the grill for a few minutes). Pour the liquid into a saucepan, add cream, wine and a little stock if desired, thicken with flour and stir in the cream. Season to taste.

Knuckle of veal is best served with dumplings and fresh salad.

● A few **variations :**
- cover the meat with sliced bacon before cooking ;
- brush on a mixture of egg and breadcrumbs before cooking ;
- or give the gravy a completely new taste by seasoning with lots of grated nutmeg.

The Italians have their own method of preparing and cooking knuckle of veal, so why not try that for a change. Here's the recipe :

Ossobucco

- 1 knuckle of veal
  1 onion
  juice of 1 lemon
  grated lemon rind
  1 cup grated cheese
  2 tomatoes
  2 tbs. tomato puree

  1 tbs. butter
  2 tbs. chopped parsley
  1-2 cups wine
  1 clove garlic
  mixed dried herbs (basil,
    rosemary, thyme, sage)

Put a few pieces of butter in the bottom of the soaked RÖMER-TOPF. Rub the knuckle with salt and pepper and sprinkle the herbs over it. Put into the RÖMERTOPF and add the peeled and quartered tomatoes and the chopped onion. Pour on the lemon juice, cover and cook in a hot oven (400 F. - Gas mark 6) for at least 2½ hours. The meat should be basted from time to time with wine. Before serving add the grated cheese to the liquid and season with garlic.

Served on its own knuckle of veal is fine for slimmers.

Veal French Style

Mix together ½ pint red wine with 1 tbs, mixed herbs (thyme, parsley, sage, a bay leaf, pinch of peppermint). Rub this mixture well into a leg of veal. Then put the meat into the soaked RÖMERTOPF, pour on the remaining liquid and cook for about 2½ hours in a hot oven (400 F. - Gas mark 6). Baste from time to time. To make the dish really perfect add a little sour cream to the liquid in the pot — delicious !

Well cooked French food is always a good way of building up a reputation of being a great cook, so here's another one to try in the RÖMERTOPF':

Ragout of Veal Bourguignon

- *1 ½ lb. shoulder of veal*   *¾ lb. mushrooms*
  ¾ lb. onions   *½ pint red wine*
  5 tbs. stock   *2 tbs. butter*
  1 tbs. flour   *½ cup cream*

Cut the meat into pieces, season with salt and pepper. Brown in hot butter. Then transfer to the soaked RÖMERTOPF, together with the onions and mushrooms. Pour on the wine and stock. Cover and cook for two hours in a hot oven (425 F. - Gas mark 7). Thicken the liquid with flour and stir in the butter. Warm the cream and add to the gravy.

Serve with boiled noodles.

If this doesn't have your family and guests drooling, then you can write them off as far as food appreciation is concerned !

Stuffed Breast of Veal

- *1 ½ lb. breast of veal*   *½ lb. mixed mince*
  2 onions   *4 tbs. breadcrumbs*
  1 egg   *1 tbs. butter*
  1 tbs. lemon juice   *¼ pint sour cream*
  salt and pepper

Rub the meat with salt and lemon juice. Make a stuffing from the mince, chopped onions, egg, breadcrumbs, salt and pepper. If necessary add a little stock or milk to obtain the right consistency. You should have the butcher cut a pocket in the meat for you — or do it yourself. Stuff the filling into this. Otherwise the meat can be rolled. Place the meat in the soaked RÖMERTOPF and scatter on it a few small pieces of butter. Cover and cook in a hot oven (400 F. - Gas mark 6) for 2 hours. Drain off the liquid and mix with the sour cream. If you like a thicker gravy stir in flour to thicken.

Serve with boiled potatoes, or noodles, and freshly cooked vegetables.

● There are several **variations** for preparing the stuffing :
- instead of ordinary minced meat use minced liver ;
- add chopped mushrooms ;
- add the juice of an orange and a little grated orange rind (do check always before simply using orange rind — or rind of other citrus fruits — that they have not been chemically treated. If you're not sure do wash very thoroughly in hot water) ;
- add 1 tbs. raisins, a little grated lemon rind and a pinch of sugar ;
- use any leftover roast meat ; just put it through the mincer and mix with a little Worcester sauce and sour cream.

Veal is an excellent meat for 'slimmers — but do keep an eye on the kind and amount of extras you eat with it (especially things like noodles !).

Veal Cutlets in Cream

● 4 veal cutlets   2 tbs. butter
  ½ pint cream   1 lemon
  salt and pepper

Fry the chops slowly in butter. Season with salt and pepper. Then transfer to the soaked RÖMERTOPF and pour the cream over them. Cover and cook for about ½ hour in a hot oven (425 F. - Gas mark 7). The cooking time will depend on the size of the cutlets. They are ready when the meat is quite tender and the cream of a smooth consistency. Before serving season with salt and pepper and the juice of half a lemon.
  Best served with rice.

Veal Cutlets in Wine

● 4 veal cutlets   10 oz. chopped onions
  10 oz. chopped carrots   1 lb. very small potatoes
  ½ pint white wine   1 lemon
  salt and pepper

Put the potatoes, carrots, onions, half the wine, the salt and pepper into the soaked RÖMERTOPF and cook for three quarters of an hour in a hot oven (425 F. - Gas mark 7). Meanwhile fry the chops lightly in a pan and then place on top of the vegetables. Sprinkle on a little salt and pepper, heat the remaining wine and pour over the meat and vegetables in the pot. Cook for a further half hour in a slightly cooler oven.

If you don't normally care for offal, here's a recipe which is designed to change your mind — and calves' liver really is a great delicacy. Try it once and see !

Calves' Liver in Wine

- 2 lb. calves' liver   6 oz. smoked bacon
  4 tomatoes   8 oz. onions
  8 oz. carrots   2 tbs. butter
  ½ pint red wine

Clean and lard the liver. Fry in the butter and transfer to the soaked RÖMERTOPF. Add the finely chopped carrots and onions and the peeled and quartered tomatoes. Sprinkle with salt and pepper and pour on the wine. Cover and cook in a hot oven (400 F. - Gas mark 6) for just under two hours. The juice can be thickened with flour to make a tasty gravy.
    Serve with mashed potatoes.

Excellent for slimmers — but give the potatoes a miss !

Ragout of Kidneys

- 6 calves' kidneys   2 tbs. dripping
  2 onions   ½ pint stock
  2 oz. chopped mushrooms   salt and pepper
  3 tbs. flour

Skin and slice the kidneys. Fry in hot fat for a few minutes. Then fry the onions too until they become transparent. Put the kidneys, onions and mushrooms in the soaked RÖMERTOPF. Cover with the stock. Cover and cook in a hot oven (400 F. - Gas mark 6) for about half an hour. Thicken the liquid with flour.

Serve with mashed potatoes.

Veal Bavarian Style

Here is a favourite recipe for veal from Southern Germany.

● 1½ lb. veal (breast,   2 tbs. butter
     shoulder, riblets)   1 carrot
1 onion   1 lb. asparagus
1 lemon   ½ tbs. chopped parsley
1 cup stock   salt and pepper
1 tbs. flour

Quickly brown the chopped onion and carrot, the parsley and the diced meat in hot butter. Then transfer to the soaked RÖMERTOPF. Sprinkle with salt and pepper and add the lemon juice. Stir the flour into the stock and pour over the meat. Cover and cook in a hot oven (425 F. - Gas mark 7) for about two hours. In the meantime wash, scrape and boil the asparagus. Remove the RÖMERTOPF from the oven. Add the asparagus to the meat and vegetables in the pot and add further seasonings to taste. Stir in a little butter.

You may, of course, serve veal prepared this way with your own favourite accompaniments — rice or potato. But since it is a Bavarian speciality, ideally it should be served with Bavarian dumplings. They are not at all difficult to make. The following is a typical traditional recipe (the sort of thing Bavarian grand-mothers know by heart).

In Germany the dumplings are made with *Griess* for which we shall have to substitute semolina (unsweetened).

Bring 2 pints of salted water to the boil. Meanwhile mix 4 eggs with ½ lb. semolina and some salt. When the water is boiling form the mixture into balls and drop gently into the water. Boil for 5 minutes. Then remove and leave in cold water for one hour. During this time the dumplings will increase considerably in size. Finally put back into boiling water for a further 15 minutes.

And as a contrast to the German, here is another French recipe :

Veal Fricandeau

- *1 lb. veal — heel or*   *1 onion*
     rump (chumpend or   *1 tbs. lemon juice*
     topside)   *2 cloves*
    1 tomato   *½ pint sour cream*
    1 tbs. chopped herbs   *1 glass white wine*
    2 oz. smoked bacon   *salt and pepper*
    1 small tin mushrooms
    a few peppercorns

Cut the meat into cubes. Season with salt and pepper and lemon juice. Cover the bottom of the soaked RÖMERTOPF with thin slices of bacon. Place the meat on top of this. Then put in the chopped onion, the peeled and quartered tomato, cloves and peppercorns. Cook for one hour in a hot oven (400 F. - Gas mark 6). Add the wine and mushrooms and cook for another hour.

Thicken with a little flour and finally stir in the cream.

Serve with rice and peas, cauliflower or asparagus — or, as a special treat, with chestnuts.

Good slimming diet — but omit the flour (and don't eat too much rice with it !)

Rolled Veal Slices

- *4 slices of veal*   *1 tbs. flour*
    2 tbs. chopped parsley   *½ tbs. chopped anchovies*
    2 oz. streaky bacon   *1 cup stock*

1 tbs. capers   lemon juice
2 onions   salt and pepper
1 tbs. butter

Beat the veal and rub with salt and pepper. Spread on the slices the chopped onion, capers, chopped bacon and parsley and roll up carefully. Tie with string or pierce with a skewer. Arrange in the soaked RÖMERTOPF and sprinkle on top the butter cut into small pieces. Stir the flour into the stock and pour this over the meat. Cover and cook in a very hot oven (475 F. - Gas mark 9) for an hour. Season the liquid with lemon juice, salt and pepper to taste.

Serve with potatoes and a green vegetable or salad.

As a general rule veal stuffed and rolled in this way should be much milder and less highly spiced than beef rolls — bear this in mind when adding seasonings.

● Here are a few suggestions for **variations :**
- chop two hard boiled eggs, mix them with a little chopped gherkin and fill the rolls with this mixture ;
- for a filling try minced beef mixed with an egg and seasoned with salt and pepper ;
- sprinkle grated cheese over the rolled slices before cooking ;
- season generously with rosemary and sage ;
- before rolling up the slices, do not fill them but simply season with salt and pepper and a few small pieces of butter ; then roll them up, place them in the soaked RÖMERTOPF and arrange around them 10 small onions (whole, skinned) and four chopped carrots ; sprinkle with flour and add ½ cup white wine and ½ cup stock.

Veal Blanquette

● 2 lbs. veal   2 oz. mushrooms
1 onion   1 carrot
2 tbs. butter   2 tbs. flour
½ cup cream   1 egg-yolk
2 tbs. chopped parsley   1 tsp. mixed herbs
1 clove   salt and pepper

Dice the meat and blanch by plunging into boiling water for 5-10 minutes. Then transfer to the soaked RÖMERTOPF. Slice the mushrooms and carrot, chop the onion and add these to the meat. Pour on the stock and add the clove and herbs. Cover and cook in a hot oven (400 F. - Gas mark 6) for 2 hours — or until meat is tender. Heat the butter in a saucepan and gradually stir in the flour. Cook for 2-3 minutes and then gradually add the liquid drained from the RÖMERTOPF. When this mixture is of an even consistency add the cream and beaten egg. Pour this mixture back over the meat, stir carefully.

Sprinkle with the chopped parsley before serving.

Veal in White Wine

- *1½ lb. veal (breast without bone)*
  1 glass white wine
  1 cup stock

  2 tbs. flour
  2 oz. mushrooms
  ½ cup cream
  2 tbs. butter

Dice the meat and sauté in a frying pan. Add the sliced mushrooms and cook together for a few minutes. Then transfer to the soaked RÖMERTOPF. Pour on the wine and cook in a hot oven (400 F. - Gas mark 6) for 2-2½ hours — until the meat is tender. Melt the butter in pan and stir in the flour, then slowly add the stock. Continue to cook until this mixture thickens and achieves an even consistency, then remove the RÖMERTOPF from the oven and pour over the meat. Add salt and pepper to taste. Finally stir in the cream and serve with buttered noodles.

Not suitable for slimmers !

Veal with Rice

- *1 lb. veal*
  2 cups rice
  1 cup grated cheese

  3 tomatoes
  curry powder
  salt and pepper

1 onion	*1 cup dried fungi*
4 cups water	*(obtainable in packets —*
2 tbs. chopped parsley	*if you can't manage to*
1 clove of garlic	*get any use chopped*
stock	*mushrooms)*

Cut the meat into slices, chop the onions and peel and slice the tomatoes. If using dried fungi they should be soaked for a few hours beforehand. Put the vegetables and rice in the soaked RÖMERTOPF and pour on 3 cups of stock. Add the crushed garlic and salt and pepper to taste. Cover and cook in a hot oven (400 F. - Gas mark 6) for just under an hour. You may need to add up to a cup more stock, so check once or twice during the cooking period to see that the rice has not dried out too much — the finished dish, however, should not be soggy! Before serving stir in the grated cheese and parsley.

For an extra dash of taste season with tabasco.

Serve with fresh salads.

Other ingredients may be added to vary the dish : peas, chopped sweet peppers, an egg yolk plus lots of fresh herbs. Or, an alternative way of 'hotting it up' a bit — stir lots of paprika-pepper into half a pint of sour cream, add crushed garlic and a chopped onion and stir this mixture into the dish before serving.

Not suitable for slimmers !

Pork

The fact that meat can be cooked in a RÖMERTOPF without any additional fat is especially important with pork. Cooked in the RÖMERTOPF pork is less fatty and therefore more digestible — and contains fewer calories — but is nevertheless deliciously tender. Try some of our recipes and see for yourself !

Roman Pot Pork

- 2 lbs. roasting pork
  1 tsp. bread crumbs
  2 tomatoes
  salt and pepper

  1 onion
  1 tsp. butter (optional)
  caraway seeds

Rub the meat with salt and pepper. Score the crackling. Put the meat, together with the chopped onion, the skinned and quartered tomatoes and the butter into the soaked RÖMERTOPF. Sprinkle bread crumbs and some caraway seeds (to taste — can be left out if you don't care for the flavour !) over the crackling. Cover and cook in a hot oven (400 F. - Gas mark 6) for 2 hours. The liquid may then be drained off, a little stock added and the mixture thickened with flour. This makes an excellent gravy. Return the RÖMERTOPF to the oven without the lid for about ten minutes or until the meat is nicely browned.

● The flavourings can be **varied** in many different ways :
- rub the meat well with rosemary before placing in the pot ;
- or add 2 cloves, 2 peppercorns and a bay leaf to the pot before placing in the oven ;
- try a Swedish alternative. Rub the pork with ground ginger before cooking and add a cup of chopped pineapple to the sauce at the end — delicious !

Pork is especially fine when cooked with sweet garnishings for a change. Instead of the onions and tomatoes add four sliced apples to the meat in the pot.

Pilaw

- 1 lb. pork (loin is best
     for this recipe)
  2 cups rice
  3 sweet peppers
  2 tbs. butter
  1 small tin tomato puree

  salt and pepper
  4 cups stock
  3 onions
  3 tbs. chopped bacon
  3 tbs. grated cheese
  paprika pepper

Heat the bacon in a frying pan and then add the butter. Cut the onion, peppers, and meat into fairly large cubes and fry them in the pan. Then transfer to the soaked RÖMERTOPF. Add the rice. Warm the stock and pour it over the ingredients in the RÖMERTOPF. Cover and cook in a hot oven (400 F. - Gas mark 6) for ¾ hour.

Before serving stir in the tomato puree and grated cheese and add salt and pepper to taste.

● There are a great many **variations** to this Balkan speciality :
- the first and most obvious one : flavour with plenty of garlic !
- mix a handful of chopped parsley into a cup of yoghurt and stir this into the pilaw before serving ;
- a very special suggestion : mix 3 beaten eggs, a finely chopped peperoni and a small glass of spirits together. Pour this mixture over the finished dish and return to the oven without the lid to allow it to brown.

Sweet and Sour Pork

● *2 largish pieces of loin*   *1 cup diced pineapple*
1 egg-yolk   *2 tsp. flour*
½ small tin tomato puree   *1 onion*
1 cup stock   *1 tsp. curry powder*
1 tsp. cornflour   *juice of ½ lemon*
salt and pepper

Cut the meat into cubes. Mix the egg-yolk, lemon juice, salt, flour and 2 tsp. pineapple juice. Dip the pieces of meat in this mixture and then fry them, together with the chopped onion, in hot butter. Then transfer to the soaked RÖMERTOPF. Mix the stock, curry powder, tomato puree, cornflour and pineapple pieces and pour this over the meat. Cover and cook in a medium oven (350 F. - Gas mark 4) for about ½ hour.

Stir in a little soy sauce before serving with boiled rice.

Not suitable for slimmers !

Pork Italian Style

When you or your family are feeling in the mood for a change, try one of the following Italian recipes for pork.

- 1 lb. pork (loin is best for this)
  1/2 lb. mushrooms
  1 clove of garlic
  1 tsp. tomato puree

  thyme, rosemary and sage
  1/2 lb. tomatoes
  1 cup sour cream
  1 tsp. anchovy butter
  salt and pepper

Cut up the meat into fairly small pieces. Peel and cut up the tomatoes and chop the mushrooms. Cover the bottom of the soaked RÖMERTOPF with the sliced ham and then add the meat in layers, alternating with the mushroom and tomato. Finish with another layer of ham. Mix together the sour cream, tomato puree, the crushed garlic clove and the herbs and pour this mixture over the meat and vegetables. Sprinkle small pieces of anchovy butter on the top (if you don't have any anchovy butter, warm some ordinary butter and mix a little anchovy paste into it). Cover and cook in a very hot oven (475 F. - Gas mark 9) for an hour.

Serve with spaghetti, fresh salad and red wine (an Italian one, of course, for preference).

Unfortunately not suitable for slimmers !

● If you have tried this dish and would like **to vary** it another time try one of these suggestions :
- add grated cheese between the layers of meat and vegetables in the pot ;
- or mix 1/2 cup grated cheese with the yolks of two eggs and pour this over the top. Sprinkle generously with chopped parsley.

Bolaggio

- 6 oz. lean pork belly
  1 onion

  4 tomatoes
  6 oz. white beans

1 clove of garlic
rosemary and thyme
12 oz. shoulder of pork
2 carrots

6 oz. white cabbage
½ pint stock
1 tsp. butter
salt and pepper

Chop the pork into cubes. Chop up the vegetables fairly small and brown them quickly in a frying pan. Then put all the ingredients into the soaked RÖMERTOPF. Cover and cook in a hot oven (425 F. - Gas mark 7) for 2 hours.

Not for slimmers !

French Liver Pie

● 1½ lb. liver
6 oz. streaky bacon
1 small glass brandy
(or calvados)
1 clove of garlic
puff pastry made with
about 6 oz. flour
(or 1 packet
deep frozen
puff pastry)

¾ lb. cooked pork
1 onion
1 tbs. butter
some dried thyme and
marjoram
salt and pepper

Roll out the pastry so that there is sufficient to line the RÖMERTOPF and for a cover. Mince the liver, pork and onion and then mix together well, plus the butter. Season this mixture with a little thyme and marjoram, the crushed garlic and salt and pepper. Stir in well, then add the brandy. Make sure all the ingredients are well combined. Then line the soaked RÖMER-TOPF with a layer of pastry and place on a layer of streaky bacon. Fill the meat mixture into this and cover with a layer of pastry (make 2 or 3 holes in the top to allow moisture to escape). Cover and cook in a hot oven (400 F. - Gas mark 6) for 1¼ hour.

Best served with fresh salad or green vegetables — and, if possible, a good wine.

Not for slimmers !

Ham with Corn

● ½ *lb. cooked ham*   *1 large tin corn*
   ½ *cup grated cheese*   *2 tbs. flour*
   2 tbs. butter   ½ *pint stock*
   2 tbs. breadcrumbs

Cut the ham into cubes. Put the ham and corn into the soaked RÖMERTOPF. Melt the butter in a saucepan and stir in the flour. Then add the stock and cook gently until an even consistency is obtained. Stir about half the breadcrumbs and cheese into this sauce and pour over the ham and corn in the RÖMERTOPF. Cover and cook for about half an hour in a hot oven (400 F. - Gas mark 6). Then remove from the oven. Mix the remaining breadcrumbs and grated cheese and sprinkle over the food in the Roman Pot. Return to the oven without the lid and cook until nicely browned on top.

Bacon with Beans

● *2 lb. bacon*   ¾ *lb. beans (dried or*
   2 onions   *tinned butter beans)*
   2 tbs. tomato puree   ½ *pint stock*

If you use dried beans soak them overnight. Cut the bacon into cubes and place in the soaked RÖMERTOPF together with the chopped onions and the beans. Stir the tomato puree into the stock and pour over the ingredients in the casserole. Season with salt and pepper to taste, cover and cook in a hot oven (400 F. - Gas mark 6) for 3 hours.

● You can **vary** this dish in several ways :

- sprinkle well with chopped parsley before serving ;
- add a chopped sweet pepper to the RÖMERTOPF before putting in the oven ;
- add a few other chopped vegetables to the dish before cooking : root vegetables, for example, mix in very well.

Not suitable for slimmers !

Bacon with Liver

● ¾ lb. sliced bacon
3 onions
½ pint stock
½ lb. liver

½ lb. mushrooms
a little freshly ground
pepper

Place a thin layer of sliced bacon in the bottom of the soaked RÖMERTOPF. Chop the onions and fry in a little hot fat in a pan. Cut the liver into fairly small pieces and slice the mushrooms. Mix the onions, mushrooms and liver together and spread a layer of this on top of the bacon. Continue adding layers of the bacon and liver and mushroom mixture — finishing with sliced bacon. Season with a little freshly ground pepper and then pour on the stock. Cover and cook in a hot oven (400 F. - Gas mark 6) for about 1 hour.

If you would like a nice crispy layer of bacon on top, remove the lid of the RÖMERTOPF and return to the oven for a further 10-15 minutes cooking time.

Knuckle of Pork with Sauerkraut

● 1 pork knuckle
(about 2 lb.)
1 baking apple
juniper berries
2 tbs. butter
1 tbs. mixed herbs

1 tin sauerkraut
(in wine)
1 bay leaf
½ onion
2 cloves
1 cup stock

The knuckle should be boiled for an hour so that it is half cooked, before you start this recipe. Put the sauerkraut in the bottom of the soaked RÖMERTOPF. Peel and core the apple and shred one half of it. Stick the cloves, a few juniper berries and the bay leaf in the other half and put all the apple on top of the sauerkraut. Pour on the stock. Chop the onions and place these with the knuckle in the centre of the RÖMERTOPF, making a shape in the sauerkraut. Cover and cook in a hot oven (400 F. - Gas mark 6) for 1½ - 2 hours. Before serving thicken the juices with the flour and stir in the butter.

Serve with potatoes.

Diet : omit the butter and flour (and forget the potatoes) and then you have an excellent protein rich meal.

● **Variations :**
- line the RÖMERTOPF with streaky bacon, put half the sauerkraut under the meat and the rest on top ; pour on ½ cup of wine instead of stock ;
- other cuts of ham or pork may be used in place of the knuckle (boiling cuts).

Spare Ribs Stuffed and Rolled

● 2½ lb. spare ribs   1 lb. dried fruit
   (get it in one piece,   1-2 cooking apples
   but have the butcher   2 tbs. sultanas
   cut through the bone)   1 tbs. chopped almonds

Soak the dried fruit and when softened mix with the chopped apple, sultanas and almonds. Spread this mixture over the meat, roll up carefully and tie. Put into the soaked RÖMERTOPF, sprinkle with a little salt, cover and cook in a very hot oven (475 F. - Gas mark 9) for 1½ - 2 hours.

Best served with boiled potatoes and a green vegetable or fresh salad.

Mutton and Lamb

Roman Pot Lamb

These quantities will serve 6-8 :

● 2½ lb. lamb
pinch of peppermint
  (or even better a sprig
  of fresh mint)
1 tbs. oil
paprika pepper

1 tbs. thyme
1 clove of garlic
1 onion
2 tbs. grated cheese
1 small tin mushrooms
salt and pepper

Rub the meat with salt and pepper, place it in the soaked RÖMERTOPF and carefully pour on a little lemon juice. Leave to stand for a time. Mix the paprika pepper (amount according to personal preference), crushed garlic, finely chopped thyme and peppermint well with the oil and rub this into the meat. Chop the mushrooms and onion and place them on the meat. Cover and cook in a hot oven (450 F. - Gas mark 8) for 1½ hours. Then stir the liquid in the casserole gently with a fork — the softened vegetables should stir in easily. Then add the grated cheese and serve.

Best served with boiled new potatoes and a green vegetable. The classic accompaniment to lamb is, of course, mint sauce :

● Mint Sauce

Mix 1 tbs. sugar, 2 tbs. chopped mint (fresh if at all possible) and 1 tbs. vinegar. A few drops of boiling water may be added to make blending easier. Leave to stand for some time before using.

For lovers of highly spiced food here is a recipe for

Lamb Curry

(not for the uninitiated)
Will give about 6 helpings :

● 2 lb. lamb	2 onions
½ cup dessicated coconut	2 cloves of garlic
1½ tsp. turmeric	a little stock
1 tsp. ground cumin	3 tbs. butter
½ tsp. chili powder	1 tsp. salt
½ tsp. ground ginger	1½ tsp. coriander

Dice the meat and place in the soaked RÖMERTOPF. Chop the onions and scatter over the meat. Crush the garlic, mix with the other seasonings, add these to the RÖMERTOPF and pour over a little stock (if the seasonings are unobtainable 2-2½ tbs. Indian curry powder may be used instead). Cover and cook in a hot oven (400 F. - Gas mark 6) for about 1½ hours — until the meat is tender. May then be thickened with a little flour and served with rice.

Not for slimmers !

Lamb Casserole

These amounts will give about 6 helpings :

● 2 lb. lamb (neck, scrag or breast)	salt and pepper
	2 onions
3 tbs. butter	1 bay leaf
1 lemon	4 tbs. flour
½ cup sour cream	½ pint milk

Clean the meat and cut into cubes. Place in the soaked RÖMERTOPF with the chopped onions, the grated rind of the lemon and the bay leaf. Season with salt and pepper to taste. Add a little water or stock (½ -1 cup). Cover and cook in a hot oven (400 F. - Gas mark 6) for about 1½ hours. Melt the butter in a saucepan and gradually stir in the flour. Use this to thicken the liquid in the RÖMERTOPF. Stir in the sour cream before serving.

Good for slimmers — without the cream.

Lamb Cutlets with Beans

● 8 lamb cutlets
½ lb. onions
½ pint stock
1 cup dried beans

6 oz. bacon
2 tbs. butter
salt and pepper

Soak the beans overnight. On the following day prepare the dish as follows. Brown the cutlets in hot butter in a frying pan, then add the chopped bacon and onions and cook together for a few minutes. Place the cutlets in the bottom of the soaked RÖMER TOPF. Stir the bacon and mushrooms from the frying pan with the beans, season with salt and pepper and spread this mixture over the meat. Pour on the stock, cover and cook in a hot oven (400 F. - Gas mark 6) for about one hour.

Not for slimmers !

Mutton with Mixed Vegetables

● 2 lb. mutton
(middle neck or breast
are the best cuts for
this recipe)
½ - ¾ lb. peas or beans
(mixed, if you like !)
¾ - 1 lb. mixed vegetables

(carrot, turnip, potato,
etc. — the vegetables
used must be firm)
½ pint stock
2 onions
2 tbs. chopped parsley
salt and pepper

Cut the meat into cubes and clean and chop the vegetables. Fry the meat in a little hot fat in a frying pan until browned. Add the onion and fry for 2-3 minutes longer. Then transfer to the soaked RÖMERTOPF and add all the other vegetables. Season with salt and pepper and pour on the stock. Cover and cook in a hot oven (400 F. - Gas mark 6) for 2½ hours. Sprinkle with chopped parsley before serving.

With the amounts given here you will have 6-8 helpings.

Not suitable for anyone watching her (or his) weight.

Lancashire Hot Pot

For six good helpings :

- 2 lb. lamb (neck -   2 onions
  scrag or middle)   1 tbs. butter
  1½ lb. potatoes   salt and pepper
  1 cup stock

Dice the meat, wash and slice the vegetables. Arrange the meat Place in the soaked RÖMERTOPF in layers, first potatoes, then meat and onions, sprinkling each with a little salt and pepper. Finish with potatoes. Pour on the stock. Cover and cook in a hot oven (400 F. - Gas mark 6) for 2½ hours. Remove the lid during the final ten minutes to allow to brown on top.

Stewed Mutton

- 1½ lb. mutton   2 carrots
  2 onions   2-3 potatoes
  1 cup stock   parsley and thyme
  bay leaf   salt and pepper

Dice the meat, wash and slice the vegetables. Arrange the meat and vegetables in the bottom of the soaked RÖMERTOPF. Sprinkle with the seasonings and pour on the stock. Cook in a moderately hot oven (375 F. - Gas mark 5) for 2 hours.

Especially delicious cooked with stew are *dumplings* which should be made as follows :

Mix about 1½ cups flour with ½ cup suet and ½ tsp. salt. Add enough water to make a firm dough. Form into balls and add to the stew half an hour before the end of the cooking time.

Braised Leg of Lamb

These quantities will give 6-8 helpings :

- 2½ lb. leg of lamb
  1 carrot
  1 lemon
  2 tbs. butter

  2 onions
  1 tomato
  1 pint of beer
  salt and pepper

Rub the meat first with salt and pepper and then with lemon juice. Leave for a short time to allow the lemon juice to seep right in and then fry on all sides in hot butter. Put into the soaked RÖMERTOPF, together with the chopped onion, carrot, the peeled and quartered tomato and the rest of the lemon juice. Cover and cook in a hot oven (450 F. - Gas mark 8) for about 2½ hours. After the meat has been cooking for about an hour pour on a little warm beer and then every half hour add some more.

Serve with potatoes and green vegetables (and a nice glass of beer !)

Leg of Lamb French Style

- 4 large slices leg of
    lamb
  1 large onion
  8 oz. smoked bacon
  1 tomato
  2 cloves of garlic
  salt and pepper

  ½ pint red wine
  ½ pint wine vinegar
  1 glass calvados
  1 tbs. butter
  mixed herbs (must
    include some tarragon)

Prepare a marinade from the wine, vinegar, the finely chopped onion, crushed garlic, herbs, salt and pepper. Leave the meat to soak in this marinade for at least 24 hours. Then cover the bottom of the soaked RÖMERTOPF with thin slices of bacon. Remove the meat from the marinade, place on the bacon with the bouquet garni and cover with another layer of bacon slices. Strain the marinade and add a cupful to the RÖMERTOPF. Then pour on the calvados. Cook in a hot oven (450 F. - Gas mark 8) for 2½ hours. Before serving add a little salt and pepper to taste and stir in the butter. Absolutely delicious — and best served with potato croquettes.

Suitable for slimmers without the potatoes.

Gigot Chasseur

Serves 6-8 :

- *1 leg of lamb*   *1 pint wine vinegar*
  2 oz. smoked bacon   *1 cup sour cream*
  1 lb. onions   *½ lemon*
  ½ lb. carrots   *5 juniper berries*
  1 tsp. butter   *1 bay leaf*
  1 tsp. flour   *salt and pepper*
  1 clove   *2 tomatoes*
  1 pint red wine

Boil the vinegar with the bay leaf, clove, salt and pepper, for about ten minutes. Then add the crushed juniper berries, the red wine and a little grated lemon rind. Marinade the meat in this liquid for about four days. Then remove, dry well and lard. Place in the soaked RÖMERTOPF. Add the skinned tomatoes and the chopped onions and carrots. Strain the marinade and pour a cupful over the meat and vegetables. Cover and cook in a hot oven (450 F. - Gas mark 8) for 2½ hours. From time to time baste with a little additional marinade. Then remove from the oven. Stir the flour into the cream and blend with the liquid in the RÖMERTOPF. Return the RÖMERTOPF to the oven without the lid to allow the meat to brown.

Serve with macaroni and fresh salad.

Without the macaroni and with a very limited amount of sauce this dish is suitable for slimmers.

Irish Stew

- 1 lb. mutton (lean, without bone)
  ½ lb. beans
  ½ carrots or turnips
  1 cup stock

  ½ lb. onions
  1 lb. potatoes
  1 tbs. chopped parsley
  salt and pepper

Clean and cut the meat and chop the vegetables. Place all in the soaked RÖMERTOPF, add salt and pepper to taste and pour on the stock. Sprinkle with the chopped parsley. Cover and cook in a hot oven (400 F. - Gas mark 6) for two hours.

Not suitable for weight-watchers !

Game

VENISON

Our suggestions for preparing this excellent, but unfortunately all-too-rare, meat in your RÖMERTOPF.

- About 2 lb. venison
  1 onion
  2 tbs. butter
  1 pint sour cream
  grated lemon rind
  salt and pepper

  ½ pint vinegar
  1 onion
  marjoram, thyme, sage
  1 bay leaf
  juniper berries

Prepare a marinade by boiling the vinegar briefly with the chopped onion and the seasonings. Leave the meat in this liquid for about three days. Then remove the meat, dry and lard. Place in the soaked RÖMERTOPF, add butter in small pieces and the marinade. Cover and cook in a very hot oven (475 F. - Gas mark 9) for 2 hours. Then carefully drain off the liquid. Return the meat to the oven — without the lid — and allow to brown. Strain the liquid through a sieve and then mix with 1 tbs. red-currant jelly, 1 tbs. mustard, 1 tbs. grated gingerbread, the sour cream and plenty of chopped parsley. Heat gently until of an even consistency. Season with salt and pepper to taste.

Serve with potatoes (or dumplings for a change), Brussels sprouts and cranberry sauce.

● Here are a few of the many possible **variations** :
- marinade the meat in red wine, or buttermilk ;
- instead of larding lay thin slices of bacon over the meat ;
- use fewer seasonings and instead add chopped gherkin to the sauce ;
- add ½ lb. mushrooms and a little tomato puree ;
- carefully peel and core a few small apples and put them to stew, whole, in the liquid with the meat.

Venison is excellent for anyone on a slimming diet.

With the quantities given here you should have sufficient meat for at least 6 good helpings.

Amsterdam Game Pie

● 2 lb. game-meat   4 tbs. butter
   (venison, hare, partridge)   1 pinch ground ginger
  rosemary, marjoram, sage   3 eggs
 ½ pint sour cream   6 oz. bacon
 ½ lb. minced veal   salt and pepper
 a little grated lemon ;
  rind

Cut the meat into large pieces and place in the soaked RÖMER-TOPF, with plenty of butter. Cover and cook in a hot oven (425 F. - Gas mark 7) for about half an hour. Then remove the lid, sprinkle salt, pepper and the other herbs (according to taste) over the meat and leave to cool. Then remove any bones. Cut up half the bacon fairly small and fry in a pan. Mix together the fried bacon, the meat from the Roman Pot, the veal, eggs and sour cream and put into the RÖMERTOPF. Cover with the rest of the bacon (sliced). Replace in the oven and cook at the same temperature for a further 2 hours. Then remove the lid and leave in for a time to brown.

Serve with potatoes and green salad.

● **Variations :**
- instead of sour cream use red wine ; then serve with a good red wine as accompaniment ;
- before browning the finished dish add a layer of grated cheese.

Weight-watchers eat without potatoes !

These amounts will give about six helpings.

HARE

Hares must be selected carefully. Very young ones are tender, but are not very tasty and hares which are too old tend to be very tough. Try and find the happy medium ! The hare does not need to be marinaded, but simply wrapped in a cloth which has been soaked in vinegar, for about two days.

For the first recipe you will need :

● *At least 2½ lbs. hare*	*3 carrots*
(a whole hare is O.K.	*1 pint red wine*
but you will need	*1 cup sour cream*
the largest RÖMERTOPF	*1 lemon*
for it)	*1 tsp. chopped parsley*
3 onions	

Season the hare well with salt and pepper and then lard (or, to save trouble, buy a frozen hare which has already been larded — these are usually good). Put the hare into the soaked RÖMERTOPF and add the chopped vegetables. Pour on the red wine. Cover and cook in a hot oven (450 F. - Gas mark 9) for 1½ hours. Strain off the liquid and stir into the juice of the lemon and the sour cream. Serve with boiled potatoes, cranberry sauce and red cabbage.

The flavour can be **varied** as follows :
- either add a few juniper berries, peppercorns, cloves and a bay leaf to the RÖMERTOPF before placing in the oven ;
- or cut up two oranges and mix them into the final sauce plus a little grated orange peel.

Jugged Hare

- *1 hare*
  1 large carrot
  4 cloves
  4 tbs. flour
  2 oz. butter
  pinch allspice

  1 large onion
  1 cup stock
  grated rind of 1 lemon
  bouquet garni,
  small glass port wine
  salt and pepper

The hare should be cleaned and jointed one day in advance and then marinaded overnight. The marinade should be prepared from 1 cup red wine, ½ cup wine vinegar, 1 small carrot and 1 small onion, both chopped fine, pinch parsley and thyme. 1 bay leaf. On the following day remove the hare from the marinade, dry and brown in a little fat in a frying pan. Then transfer to the soaked RÖMERTOPF. Clean and chop the vegetables and add them, plus all the seasonings and the vegetables from the marinade, to the hare. Pour on the stock. Cover and cook in a moderate oven (375 F. - Gas mark 5) for about two hours or until the hare is tender. Drain off the liquid into a saucepan. Mix together the butter and flour and blend carefully into the liquid, heating gently and stirring continually until the flour thickens and an even consistency is obtained. Then add the port wine and pour over the hare.

Serve with boiled potatoes, forcemeat balls and redcurrant jelly.

RABBIT

Rabbit is a meat which is sometimes a little despised — but unjustly so. It is good value and cooked with a little care makes an excellent dish. If you don't normally eat rabbit, do try it for once !

Here are two recipes to start off with. For the first you will need :

- *1 rabbit*
  1 cup red wine
  1 tsp. tomato puree
  a little sugar
  a little rosemary
  1 tsp. marmelade

  6 oz. bacon
  1 cup cream
  bouquet garni
  1 clove of garlic
  salt and pepper

Clean the rabbit and rub with salt and pepper. Cover the bottom of the soaked RÖMERTOPF with a thin layer of bacon slices. Then put in the rabbit and cover with another layer of bacon. Cook in a very hot oven (450 F. - Gas mark 9) for about 40 minutes, without any liquid. Then add the bouquet garni, the crushed garlic, tomato puree, rosemary and the wine — which should be first slightly warmed (be careful here — otherwise the hot RÖMERTOPF will crack !) — and the cream. Cook for a further two hours in a hot oven (425 F. - Gas mark 7). The liquid may be thickened with a little flour before serving.

Serve with French fried potatoes.

In the second stage of cooking try for a change just pouring red wine over the rabbit and then adding chopped mushrooms and tomatoes.

Rabbit in Beer

- *1 rabbit*
  1 onion
  a little thyme

  1 cup beer
  4 oz. bacon
  1 tsp. chopped parsley

Divide the rabbit into 4-8 pieces and soak overnight in a weak solution of vinegar. On the following day remove, dry and brown quickly in a little hot fat in a frying pan, together with the chopped onion and bacon. Then transfer to the soaked RÖMERTOPF. Add the parsley and thyme and pour on the beer. Cook for about 2 hours in a hot oven (425 F. - Gas mark 7).

Serve with French fried potatoes.

Rabbit is excellent for slimmers — but be careful with the additional vegetables. Potatoes should be left out, of course !

Poultry

Nowadays chicken has become one of our most popular foods. It's easy to prepare, economical and very tasty. When prepared simply chicken makes a good satisfying meal ; add a little cream, white wine, or even brandy, and it can become something really special. Whether you like your chicken roast whole, or jointed and casseroled, you can of course prepare it in your RÖMERTOPF. The following includes a selection of recipes for chicken from all over the world. But there are lots more. Perhaps you already have a few special ones of your own ? Why not write and let us know ?

Chicken will fit easily into the smaller RÖMERTOPF, but for larger birds, for turkey, goose and large ducks, Bay produce an extra large Roman Pot — you can get a 14 lb. turkey into it.

CHICKEN (basic recipe)

● *1 chicken*
  1 tbs. butter
  salt and pepper

Rub the chicken with salt and pepper and brush on a little melted butter. Put into the soaked RÖMERTOPF. Cover and cook

in a hot oven (400 F. - Gas mark 6) for about 1¼ hours.
Serve with French fried potatoes and fresh salad.

If you like your chicken really crisp and brown then put it back into the oven without the cover, for a further 10-15 minutes. An added delicacy is to sprinkle it with grated cheese before returning to the oven.

To prepare a gravy add a little stock to the juice from the chicken and thicken this with a little flour.

For an extra special taste pour a third of a cup of dry white wine over the chicken before putting into the oven.

Chicken in Burgundy

- 2 chickens
- 2 oz. smoked bacon
- 1 onion
- 1 small tin mushrooms
- 1 cup burgundy
- 1 small glass brandy
- salt and pepper
- ½ 1 cup sour cream
- 2 oz. butter
- lemon juice
- 2 tbs. parsley
- 1 bay leaf
- thyme, tarragon, nutmeg

Wash, then rub the chicken with salt and pepper and a little lemon juice. Put into the soaked RÖMERTOPF. Cover with slices of bacon. Mix the cream and burgundy and pour over the chicken, then add the seasonings. Cook in a very hot oven (475 F. - Gas mark 9) for an hour. Then pour off the sauce carefully and return the chickens to the oven, without the cover, to brown. Strain the liquid through a sieve. Add the mushrooms and butter and thicken with flour. For the final delightful touch of flavour add the brandy.

Diet : leave out the butter and bacon and replace the sour cream with yoghurt.

These amounts will serve six.

Stuffed Chicken

Proceed as described in the basic recipe above but before putting the chicken into the oven stuff it with one of the following mixtures :

1. Mix the following together well :

the heart and liver of the chicken, finely chopped	*½ cup finely chopped ham*
	½ cup white wine
	½ bay leaf
1 finely chopped onion	*a little thyme and sage*
1 crushed clove of garlic	*salt and pepper*

2. Mix the following together well :

the chicken liver, finely chopped	*½ - 1 cup breadcrumbs*
	2-3 oz. dripping, warmed to soften
a little grated lemon rind	*1 tbs. chopped parsley*
1 egg, beaten	*salt and pepper*

3. Drain and chop a small tin of mushrooms. Chop one onion and fry with 1 tbs. chopped parsley in a little hot butter. Mix with the mushrooms, add salt and pepper.

Another way of treating the chicken is to brush it outside with a fairly strongly seasoned paste. For example : mix together well 2 tbs. white flour, 1 tbs. butter. 1 tbs. curry powder and 1 tbs. lemon juice.

A very simple idea — prick a lemon and put inside the chicken before cooking. During cooking the lemon will give off a unique aroma and impart a very special flavour to the chicken.

Chicken Paprika

1 chicken	*4 oz. smoked bacon*
½ onion	*1 tsp. paprika pepper*
1 tbs. chopped parsley	*½ pint sour cream*
2 tsp. tomato puree	*salt*
1 cup stock	

Divide the chicken into pieces. Rub in salt and roll in paprika pepper. Fry the sliced bacon. Place the bacon slices in the bottom of the soaked RÖMERTOPF and on them the chicken, chopped onion and stock. Cook in a hot oven (400 F. - Gas mark 6) for 1½ hours. Stir in the cream and thicken with a little flour. Sprinkle with chopped parsley before serving.

Serve with rice.

● **Variations :**
- sprinkle the cooked chicken with grated cheese and return to the oven for a further ten minutes until brown ;
- add a few chopped mushrooms at the beginning ;
- add 2-3 chopped carrots at the beginning ;
- add ½ glass white wine.

Diet : use yoghurt instead of cream and don't thicken with flour.

Tokio Chicken

● *1 chicken*
1 egg
paprika pepper
2 tbs. breadcrumbs
lemon juice
6 oz. minced meat

1 small tin morello
cherries
2 oz. chopped almonds
2 tbs. oil
salt and pepper

Rub the chicken with salt, pepper and a little lemon juice. Make a stuffing from the breadcrumbs, minced meat, egg, almonds and stoned cherries. Fill this into the chicken, brush the bird with oil and sprinkle with paprika pepper. Place in the soaked RÖMERTOPF and cook in a very hot oven (475 F - Gas mark 9) for 1½ hours. Drain off the liquid into a saucepan, add the juice from the cherries, thicken and flavour with sugar and cinnamon.

Serve with potato croquettes and mixed fresh salad.

Before putting in the oven the chicken may be covered with slices of bacon — in fact, if the chicken is very lean, this is advisable.

A delightful flavour will be obtained if a glass of white wine is added before cooking. This will be completely absorbed by the chicken.

Chicken Fricassee Marseillaise

- *1 chicken*
  1 sweet pepper
  4 tbs. chicken stock
  garlic
  salt and pepper

  4 tomatoes
  3 tbs. white wine
  1 tbs. lemon juice
  thyme

Joint the chicken, then sauté briefly in hot butter. Transfer to the soaked RÖMERTOPF. Peel and cut up the tomatoes, cut the pepper into strips, crush the garlic and add these to the chicken. Mix the wine and stock with the salt, pepper, thyme and lemon juice and pour this over the chicken. Cook in a very hot oven (475 F. - Gas mark 9) for about 1½ hours.

Serve with rice and fresh salad.

Diet : without the rice this is an excellent dish for slimmers.

For those who like their food highly spiced here is a speciality from India :

Calcutta Chicken

- *1 chicken*
  3 tbs. butter
  1 tbs. ground ginger
  juice of 1 lemon
  ½ pint sour cream
  mango chutney

  2 oranges
  1 tbs. curry powder
  1 egg yolk
  a little sugar
  salt and pepper
  grated nutmeg

Cut the chicken into pieces. Rub with salt and pepper, sprinkle on the lemon juice and leave to stand for a time to allow the lemon juice to soak in. Put a few small pieces of butter in the bottom of the soaked RÖMERTOPF and lay the chicken on them. Cook in a very hot oven (475 F. - Gas mark 9) for 40 minutes, Then add the curry powder, some grated nutmeg, salt, sugar, pepper and a few more drops of lemon juice. Peel and cut up the oranges and put them in too. Cover and cook for a further hour. Then remove the cover and cook for a final ten minutes. Finally stir in the sour cream and thicken with the egg-yolk.

Serve with rice and mango chutney.

Diet : O.K. — but not too much rice !

With the amounts given above, the chicken will not be too hot. The curry powder can be increased or decreased according to taste.

Chicken Sirikit

● 1 boiling fowl
1 pint yoghurt
bouquet garni
1 tbs. butter
1 egg-yolk

2 tbs. lemon juice
1 tbs. curry powder
2 cloves of garlic
1 tbs. flour
salt and pepper

Clean the chicken and rub with salt, pepper and a little lemon juice. Cut into pieces, and place in the soaked RÖMERTOPF. Add the yoghurt, bouquet garni, crushed garlic and curry powder. Cook in a hot oven (450 F. - Gas mark 8) for 1½ - 2 hours, until the chicken is tender. The length of time will depend on the age of the bird. Take the pot from the oven and remove the chicken from the liquid. Remove the meat from the bones and rinse under running cold water. Strain the liquid from the pot through a sieve and throw away the bouquet garni and the hardened lumps of yoghurt. Add more curry powder and lemon juice to taste. Then stir in the butter and egg-yolk and thicken with the flour. Replace the meat in the liquid and put back into the oven for a few minutes longer.

Serve with rice.

Excellent for slimmers — but go easy on the rice !

Parisian Chicken Pie

● *1 chicken*
2 tbs. butter
2 small tins mushrooms
small jar stoned olives
3 eggs
1 packet frozen puff
pastry

2 tbs. flour
¾ pint white wine
salt
freshly ground black
pepper
½ lb. wiener (or other
small, firm sausages)

The unpleasant thing about this recipe is that the chicken has to be boned before it is cooked — tiresome though this is, it's necessary, and worth it. So do this first. Then put the chicken pieces into the soaked RÖMERTOPF with the butter. Cook for half an hour in a very hot oven (475 F. - Gas mark 9). Remove the pot from the oven, add the warmed wine, chopped sausages, mushrooms, olives, salt and pepper. The eggs should in the meantime have been hard boiled and sliced. Place the slices on top of the chicken and cover with a layer of puff pastry. Replace the lid and cook for a further hour.

Slimmers may enjoy this dish only in very limited quantities !

Chicken and Olive Casserole

● *1 chicken*
1 small tin stoned olives
4 tbs. butter
1 onion

2 tomatoes
2 tbs. tomato puree
a little basil

Cut the chicken into pieces. Fry the onion in hot butter and add the chicken and brown a little on all sides. Transfer to the soaked RÖMERTOPF. Add the peeled and quartered tomato the basil and olives. Cover and cook in a hot oven (400 F. - Gas mark 6) for 1½ hours. Stir the tomato puree into the liquid and thicken with a little flour.

May be improved with sour cream.

Chicken with Corn

- 1 chicken
  1 large can corn
  2 oz. butter
  1 small tin mushrooms

  1 onion
  ½ cup wine
  chopped parsley
  salt and pepper

Joint the chicken and brown in a little hot butter with the chopped onion. Transfer to the soaked RÖMERTOPF. Add the corn and mushrooms and pour over the wine. Cover and cook in a hot oven (400 F. - Gas mark 6) for 1½ hours. Season with salt and pepper. Sprinkle with chopped parsley before serving.

Chicken in Madeira

For six helpings you will need :

- 2 small (and tender !)
     chickens
  ½ tbs. lemon juice
  1 clove of garlic
  1 glass Madeira
  ½ cup stock

  1 tbs. tomato puree
  2 tbs. butter
  1 bay leaf
  4 oz. mushrooms
  salt and pepper

Clean and joint the chicken (leave the pieces fairly large) and fry quickly in hot butter. When browned on all sides transfer to the soaked RÖMERTOPF. Add the sliced mushrooms, crushed garlic, bay leaf, salt and pepper. Stir the lemon juice and tomato puree into the stock and pour this over the chicken. Cover and cook in a hot oven (400 F. - Gas mark 6) for about three quarters of an hour — if the chickens really are young this should be quite enough. Stir in the Madeira before serving.

Serve with rice or boiled noodles with butter.

O.K. for slimmers — without the rice or noodles !

Chicken Blanquette

● *1 chicken*
1 cup chicken stock
1 egg-yolk
salt and pepper

1 onion
½ cup cream
bouquet garni

Joint the chicken, and blanch by plunging into boiling water for a few minutes. Then transfer to the soaked RÖMERTOPF and add the chopped onion, the bouquet garni and salt and pepper to taste. Pour on the stock, cover and cook in a hot oven (400 F. - Gas mark 6) for about 1¼ hours — until meat is tender. Then drain off the stock and stir into the cream and egg-yolk. Pour this over the chicken and serve with rice.

Not for slimmers !

● **Variations :**
- use red wine instead of stock ;
- add 4 oz. sliced mushrooms to the RÖMERTOPF before cooking ;
- sprinkle generously with chopped parsley before serving ;
- add 1 chopped carrot and a piece of chopped celery to RÖMERTOPF at beginning.

TURKEY

● *1 turkey*
2 tbs. butter

salt and pepper
stock

Rub the turkey well with salt and pepper. Put small pieces of butter in the soaked RÖMERTOPF and lay in the turkey. Add more butter on top. Pour on a little stock and cook for 2½ hours in a hot oven (400 F. - Gas mark 6). The length of time will depend on the weight and the age of the turkey. The liquid from the bird may be thickened to make gravy.

To be really delicious, of course, a turkey needs to be stuffed. Here is a small selection of possible stuffings :

1. Chestnut stuffing : heat 2 lb. chestnuts in the oven until the shells and skins can be easily removed. Then put them in a saucepan and barely cover with stock. Cook slowly until tender. Rub through a sieve and then mix with 6 oz. breadcrumbs, 1 tbs. chopped parsley, 6 oz. cooked minced meat (or chopped bacon), salt and pepper to taste and enough warmed butter to give the right consistency.

2. Fry 3 tbs. chopped bacon with the chopped liver of the turkey, plus a little crushed garlic. Mix with 1½ cups breadcrumbs. 2 tbs. chopped parsley, 2 tbs. vinegar, 4 tbs. butter, 2 cups boiled and mashed potatoes (or use half potatoes and half chestnuts). Season with a little grated nutmeg, thyme, marjoram and salt and pepper. If necessary add a little stock to obtain the desired consistency. Chopped prunes may also be added to this stuffing.

3. Chop the liver and heart of the turkey and mix with ½ lb. minced meat and ½ lb. chopped mushrooms. Season with salt and pepper.

4. Mix skinned and chopped chestnuts with chopped bacon. Fry in a little hot butter ; flavour with a small glass of spirits.

5. Hunter's Stuffing : make from minced meat and breadcrumbs, moistened with 2 tbs. butter and a little stock. Season with marjoram, juniper berries and thyme. Cover the turkey when stuffed with slices of bacon and then pour over 1 glass red wine. Add a few chopped mushrooms to the RÖMERTOPF.

The turkey can alternatively be served with a sauce. For example : melt 2 tbs. butter in a saucepan and stir in 2 tbs. flour. Cook for a few minutes until it begins to turn brown, then remove from the heat and carefully stir in enough stock to obtain a creamy consistency. Add one or more tbs. mustard (according to taste !) A few cocktail cherries may also be stirred into this sauce. Or, after thickening the liquid in the RÖMERTOPF with flour, add curry powder and ginger. Stir in a few chopped mandarin slices and chopped pineapple. Serve with rice.

Or, cook the *turkey* in the following way *with vegetables* :

Put 1 lb. Brussels sprouts, 1 lb. skinned tomatoes, ½ lb. mushrooms, 2 chopped onions in the soaked RÖMERTOPF. Sprinkle with mixed herbs. Put the turkey on top. Mix 3 tbs. fat with pepper and brush this on the bird. Cover and cook in a hot oven (450 F. - Gas mark 8) for about 2½ hours, depending on the age of the bird. Remove the turkey and keep in a warm place. Make gravy with a little stock, flour and gravy salt, then stir in the liquid and vegetables from the RÖMERTOPF.

Serve with boiled potatoes or dumplings.

Another way of preventing the turkey from becoming too dry during cooking is to cover it with aluminium foil.

Because of the low fat content turkey is excellent for slimmers.

Turkey can be served with boiled, fried or roast potatoes, and with a green vegetable. Especially good, for a change, with red cabbage, onions or pumpkin.

GOOSE

The goose should be cleaned, rubbed with salt and pepper and laid breast down in the soaked RÖMERTOPF. Goose is not supposed to brown at all during the first stage of cooking, so that it doesn't dry out — this is one of grandmother's golden rules. Cover and cook for two hours in a hot oven (450 F. - Gas mark 8). Then remove the cover and for the rest of the cooking time baste the goose every ten minutes, with its own juice and with cold water alternately. After a further half hour's cooking, turn the goose over and cook for half an hour more. The finished goose will be delightfully tender and beautifully crispy brown.

Goose is, of course, very fat, but you can reduce the fat content during cooking by pricking the bird in the most fatty parts (thighs, etc.) with a needle to allow the fat to run out.

There are many delicious stuffings for goose. Here are a few

suggestions to start your mouth watering :
- Skin 1½ lbs. chestnuts and boil gently until soft. Mix with 6 oz. chopped pineapple.
- Mix 2 lb. chopped cooking apples with ½ lb. sultanas.
- Mix together well 1 lb. mashed potatoes, 1 lb. minced meat, ½ lb. raisins or sultanas and 2 shredded apples.
- Boil 8 oz. rice until it is half cooked. Then mix with 8 oz. chopped liver, 2 eggs, 1 finely chopped onion, the chopped liver and heart of the goose, salt and pepper.
- Shred 4 cooking apples and mix with 1 cup prunes, 1 cup raisins, some gingerbread which has been soaked in milk, a few juniper berries, half a finely chopped onion, salt and pepper.
- Soak 1 lb. prunes for several hours, then stone. Peel, core and slice 2 lb. apples. Cook for about 2 hours in a saucepan with 3 oz. sugar and a little butter and water. Stir well.
- Mix 4-5 finely chopped onions, 4 oz. breadcrumbs, 2 tbs. butter (warmed to mix), 1-2 tsp. sage, salt and pepper.

Goose is usually served with roast potatoes (boiled, if you prefer) and a green vegetable. Cranberry sauce or red-currant jelly are also delicious extras. Or, for a change, try serving it the traditional German way with dumplings and red cabbage stewed in bacon fat with apples.

For a complete change try the following recipe for goose :

Strassburg Goose Casserole

● 2 lb. goose
1 cup apple juice
  (or try cider)
1 quince
3 cloves
1 bay leaf
salt and pepper

1 tin sauerkraut
  (in wine)
2 tbs. goose fat
1 glass calvados
1 onion
1 tbs. honey

Cut the goose into pieces and fry until browned on all sides. Season with salt and pepper. Put the sauerkraut in the bottom of the soaked RÖMERTOPF. Cut the onion in halves and stick with the cloves and bay leaf. Place on top of the sauerkraut. Peel and stone the quince, chop and spread in the RÖMERTOPF. Stir the honey into the apple juice or cider and pour this over the mixture. Put the fried meat on top. Cover and cook in a very hot oven (475 F. - Gas mark 9) for 3 hours. Then remove the onions. Serve the meat separately. Stir the sauerkraut with a fork to make sure that the quince and the juices from the meat are well blended and then flavour with the calvados.

As you can see, the RÖMERTOPF is full of good things long before the goose gets there ! With a large RÖMERTOPF, of course, the recipe may be made with larger portions of goose — but don't forget to increase the other ingredients accordingly.

In Alsace this is served with potatoes which are prepared in the following way :
Wash carefully and then cut into two lengthways. Place them in the oven, sprinkle with salt, caraway seeds and small pieces of butter and leave to cook until soft.

This recipe is not suitable for slimmers !

These quantities should provide enough for six good helpings.

DUCK

Duck can be prepared as goose. The cooking time will be a little shorter — about 2 hours altogether.
But if you'd like a change from roast and stuffed duck, here are a few other suggestions.

Brussels Duck

● *1 duck*
1 tbs. cornflour
½ cup white wine
pinch cinnamon
½ lb. morello cherries

½ tbs. cinnamon
½ cup stock
salt and pepper
sugar

Cook the duck as usual. During the cooking pour on a little stock from time to time. Then remove the duck from the pot and pour the liquid into a saucepan. Add the cinnamon, sugar, wine and cherries (which have been stoned and, unless very soft, boiled a little). Thicken with flour.

Serve with potato croquettes or French fried potatoes.

Duck with Pineapple

After cooking mix the liquid from the RÖMERTOPF with 1 cup chopped pineapple, a little curry powder, ground ginger and a small glass of brandy.

Duck with Orange Sauce

Cook the duck without any stuffing. Mix the liquid in the RÖMERTOPF with the juice and grated rind of 1 orange and half a lemon, the chopped orange peel and a pinch of sugar. Thicken with cornflour and season to taste.

Duck with pineapple or orange is best served with boiled rice into which 2 or 3 tbs. chopped parsley are stirred immediately before serving.

Duck with Fruit and Sauerkraut

● *1 duck.*   *salt and pepper*
  ½ lb. mixed fruit   *1½ lb. sauerkraut*
  (tinned will do)   *½ pint stock*
  1 sweet pepper   *1 tbs. cornflour*

Mix the sauerkraut with the fruit and finely chopped pepper. Put into the soaked RÖMERTOPF. Cut the duck into pieces, rub in a little salt and pepper and place on top of the sauerkraut. Pour on the stock (the stock should be nice and beefy — so if necessary add an extra beef bouillon cube). Cover and cook in a hot oven (400 F. - Gas mark 6) for about 2 hours. Then remove the meat and place to keep warm. (It can be put under the grill for a few minutes to brown, if desired). Thicken the sauerkraut mixture with a little flour. Season to taste.

Serve with dumplings.

Duck Niçois

● 1 duck
   12 oz. stoned olives
   2 small glasses wine
   salt and pepper
   thyme

   2 lb. tomatoes
   2 small glasses brandy
   1 clove garlic
   rosemary

Rub the duck with salt, pepper and garlic and place in the soaked RÖMERTOPF. Slice the olives, peel and quarter the tomatoes and place in the RÖMERTOPF with the duck. Sprinkle with rosemary and thyme. Pour on the brandy and wine. Cover and cook in a very hot oven (475 F. - Gas mark 9) for about 2 hours.

WILD DUCK

Wild duck makes a delicious change from the home and farm bred ones. It contains much less fat and should be covered with slices of bacon before cooking. In particular be careful not to overcook wild duck, or it will lose its special flavour.

PHEASANT

Pheasant can be treated in the same way for roasting in the RÖMERTOPF as chicken. It is particularly fine if browned a little in a frying pan before being put into the RÖMERTOPF. Pour a little sour cream over it before cooking and then blend more cream into the liquid before serving.

PIGEONS

Pigeons are a delicacy which are all too rarely enjoyed nowadays. Yet they once enjoyed a much greater popularity among lovers of good food. Here are two suggestions for how to prepare them. Try to obtain young pigeons, these are infinitely better, not just because of the tenderness, but also the flavour. If, however, you do have an older bird, boil it for an hour before continuing as follows :

Stuffed Pigeon

- *4 pigeons*
  4 eggs
  a little grated nutmeg
  salt and pepper

2 tbs. chopped parsley
3 tbs. butter
2 breakfast rolls

Rub the pigeons with salt inside and out. Soak the rolls, squeeze out the excess moisture, then mix with the parsley and the chopped hearts and livers of the pigeons. Fry quickly in butter. Then add the beaten eggs, season with salt, pepper and grated nutmeg. Stuff the pigeons with this mixture and place in the soaked RÖMERTOPF. Add a few small pieces of butter, cover and cook in a hot oven (400 F. - Gas mark 6) for 1½ hours.

Serve with boiled potatoes and fresh salad.

Pigeon Pot

- *4 pigeons*
  1 onion
  1 tbs. cornflour
  1 cup stock
  thyme

2 oz. smoked bacon
1 tbs. chopped parsley
juice of ½ lemon
salt and pepper

Cover the bottom of the soaked RÖMERTOPF with thinly sliced bacon. Cut the pigeons into pieces and place on the bacon. Scatter over them the finely chopped onion, parsley, a little thyme, lemon juice, salt and pepper. Pour on the stock, cover and cook in a hot oven (400 F. - Gas mark 6) for 1½ hours. A little white wine and /or butter may be added if desired.

● **Variations :**
- cover the pigeons with bacon slices before cooking ;
- add sour cream to the gravy ;
- boil a few chopped mushrooms, asparagus, cauliflower and peas for a short time and add them to the dish about ten minutes before the dish is ready ;
- marinade the pigeons overnight in diluted vinegar with a chopped onion, a few juniper berries and a bay leaf.

PARTRIDGE

(A delicacy you really must try when the birds are in season.)

- *3 young partridges*
  1 tbs. butter
  1 bay leaf
  a little thyme
  ½ tbs. mixed herbs
  ½ cup red wine

4 oz. smoked bacon
1 tbs. lemon juice
2-3 peppercorns
1 onion
salt
½ cup sour cream

Rub the partridges well with salt and lemon juice. Chop the hearts and livers of the partridges and mix with the butter, lemon juice and herbs. Stuff the birds with this mixture and put into the soaked RÖMERTOPF. Sprinkle a few more herbs on top. Cover with thin slices of bacon. Put on the lid and cook in a hot oven (450 F. - Gas mark 8) for about 1½ hours. Can be finished off with 15 minutes under the grill to brown. During the cooking period pour over a little red wine from time to time.

Partridge in Mushroom and Madeira Sauce

Prepare the partridges as above. Strain the liquid from the birds through a sieve. Add a cup of madeira and a small tin of mushrooms. Thicken with a little flour.

Partridges are to be highly recommended to anyone on a slimming diet.

Leftovers

At the end of this section on meat I would like to add two more very practical, but also very, tasty recipes. These are two suggestions for using up leftovers. For the first one beef would be best (but is not absolutely essential) ; for the second you can use any sort of roast meat.

Casserole for Leftovers — 1

- *1 lb. cooked beef*
  2 onions
  ¼ pint white wine
  ½ cup breadcrumbs

  ½ lb. mushrooms
  3 tbs. butter
  3 tbs. chopped parsley
  2 tbs. tomato puree

Chop the onions, slice the mushrooms and fry for a few moments in about half the butter. Cut the meat into smallish pieces and place in the bottom of the soaked RÖMERTOPF. Spread the onions and mushrooms on top of the meat. Then stir the parsley and tomato puree into the white wine and pour over the ingredients already in the RÖMERTOPF. Cover and cook in a moderate oven (375 F. - Gas mark 5) for about 40 minutes. Meanwhile carefully stir the breadcrumbs into the butter (the butter may be warmed a little to make this easier, but should not become runny). Spoon the butter and breadcrumbs over the top of the food in the Roman Pot, then return to the oven without the lid, until the top is nicely browned.

Serve with potatoes and green vegetables.

- As a **variation**, you can beat 1-2 eggs and pour this over this dish before putting back into the oven to brown.

Served without potatoes, this dish can easily fit into a slimming diet.

Casserole for Leftovers — 2

- ½ lb. leftovers from
    the roast
  1 large apple
  1 lb. potatoes
  4 oz. butter

  salt and pepper
  2 onions
  ½ tin green beans
    (or peas or asparagus)
  1 cup grated cheese

Spread small pieces of butter in the bottom of the soaked RÖMERTOPF. Add the ingredients to the Roman Pot in layers: first the meat, then the sliced apple, on top of this the vegetable and finally the sliced potatoes (can be either raw or boiled — if you have boiled potatoes over, you can use them up here too). Season with salt and pepper and add a few more pieces of butter. Cook for about two hours (length will partly be affected by whether you use raw or cooked potatoes) in a very hot oven (450 F. - Gas mark 8). Before serving stir the ingredients carefully with a fork so that they are well mixed. Sprinkle with the grated cheese.

Not for slimmers !

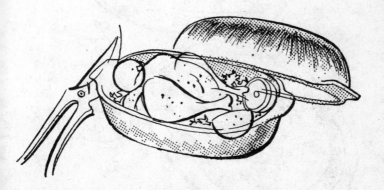

THE FISH RÖMERTOPF

If you are a lover of fish you will no doubt already be a delighted owner of the special RÖMERTOPF for fish. This is one of the latest models and was designed individually to fill a gap in the first range. A nicely cooked piece of fish is a great delicacy but — as every cook knows — its preparation is not entirely without problems. The first Roman Pot enthusiasts realized this. The characteristic smell of fish clings to almost every material, despite any amount of washing, and in the case of the RÖMERTOPF it penetrated into the pores, so that with every dish cooked afterwards in the pot the eater also enjoyed the slight tang of fish ! Of course, experts already had their one RÖMERTOPF which they reserved just for cooking fish — but even then the shape wasn't quite right. So we put our heads together and the result was a special earthenware casserole for fish. Longer and shallower than the other models, its shape is ideal, and it is decorated with an appropriate motif. The rest is up to you !

Our basic recipe follows — but before starting do bear in mind the fundamentals about cooking fish. Don't leave it lying around in water, as this will ruin the quality and flavour, but wash it under running water. Don't add salt until just before serving. And if you like your fish nice and firm, white and with an extra good flavour, sprinkle on lemon juice before cooking (this also helps to reduce the smell).

Steamed Fish

Pour fish stock into the bottom of the soaked RÖMERTOPF (about ¼-½ inch deep). Then add the fish, cover and cook for about 35 minutes in a hot oven (400 F. - Gas mark 6).

The fish stock can be prepared from 1 cup water which has been boiled for about 20 minutes with a little vinegar and salt, 1 chopped onion, 1 bay leaf and 2 cloves.

For a special touch of flavour, don't use this ordinary fish stock. Just put your fish into the soaked RÖMERTOPF, sprinkle a few small pieces of butter on it and then pour on ½ cup of white wine. Cook in a hot oven (400 F. - Gas mark 6) for 35 minutes. Ready — delicious !

Fish is also excellent served with melted butter poured over it. If you like this then cook your fish with just a few small pieces of butter but without any extra liquid. Prepared like this all the flavour and goodness stays right in the fish — and not in the liquid !

Deep-frozen Fish Fillets

- 2 lb. frozen fish
  1 lemon
  1 tbs. mixed dried herbs

  paprika pepper
  mustard
  salt

Thaw out the fish. Mix together the juice of the lemon, a little paprika pepper, salt and mustard to taste. Spread this mixture evenly on the fish and place in the soaked RÖMERTOPF. Sprinkle with the herbs (or use finely chopped vegetables for a change). Cover and cook for about one hour in a hot oven (400 F. - Gas mark 6). The liquid from the pot can be thickened with sour cream, seasoned with herbs and served as a sauce with the fish.

This is an excellent dish for slimmers.

Fish Fillets with Mushrooms

- 1 lb. fish
  ½ lb. tomatoes
  4 oz. smoked bacon

  1 tbs. butter
  1 tbs. tomato puree
  1 lb. mushrooms

1 tbs. lemon juice	*1 onion*
1 cup white wine	*salt and pepper*

Put a layer of fish in the bottom of the soaked RÖMERTOPF. Then add a layer each of sliced bacon, sliced mushrooms and sliced tomatoes. Chop the onion and sprinkle this on the top. Then finish off with another layer of fish. Stir the lemon juice, tomato puree, salt and pepper into the wine and pour this over the fish. Cover and cook in a hot oven (425 F. - Gas mark 7) for about 40 minutes.

Serve with toast or boiled potatoes.

Excellent for slimmers — without the toast and potatoes.

Fish Fricassee

● *1½ lb. fish*	*1 cup red wine*
1 tbs. butter	*1 tbs. flour*
1 gherkin	*2 tbs. chopped chives*
1 glass yoghurt	*1 tbs. mustard*
1 onion	*1 tbs. cranberry sauce*

Melt the butter in a saucepan and stir in the flour. Add water, bring to the boil and allow to thicken. Then remove from the heat and stir in the cranberries, mustard, and the chopped onion. Add the red wine. Add another cup of water and pour into the soaked RÖMERTOPF. Cut the fish into cubes and place gently in the sauce. Cover and cook in a hot oven (400 F. - Gas mark 6) for about 40 minutes. Before serving stir in the yoghurt and chopped gherkin and sprinkle with the chives.

Serve with boiled potatoes.

Served alone this fricassee is excellent for slimmers.

Fish Goulash

- 1 lb. fish (cleaned and
    boned)
  ½ pint white wine
  paprika pepper

  salt
  1 lb. onions
  3 tbs. oil
  2 tbs. lemon juice

First brush the inside of the soaked RÖMERTOPF with a little of
the cooking oil. Chop the onions and separate the fish into
flakes with a fork. Put half the onions in the bottom of the pot
and then half the fish on top of them. Sprinkle well with
paprika pepper. Then put in another layer of onions and finish
with the rest of the fish. Season with salt and pour on the rest
of the oil and the lemon juice. Cook in a hot oven (425 F. - Gas
mark 7) for one hour. Then add the white wine and cook for a
further ten minutes.

This is delicious simply served with slices of freshly toasted
white bread. Or it can be served with rice.

● The dish can be **varied** in a great many ways and once you
have tried it you will no doubt find favourite variations of your
own. Here are a few suggestions to start with :
- use fewer onions and make up the amount with tomatoes. Mix
the two together before putting in the pot and season well with
rosemary and a crumbled bay leaf ;
- boil 1 lb. potatoes and mash them. Then mix well with an egg
and a little butter and season with grated nutmeg. Add layers of
this potato mixture between the layers of fish and onions.
Cooked with potato like this the fish goulash is a completely
satisfying meal in itself ;
- add a little less wine before returning to the oven for the final
ten minutes cooking time. Then, at the end, stir together ¼ pint
white wine and ¼ pint sour cream with a few mixed herbs to
taste. Pour this mixture over the finished goulash and sprinkle
generously with chopped parsley ;
- make a sauce from ½ pint sour cream seasoned with horse-
radish (about 2 tbs. — but this can be varied according to
personal taste), a little sugar, salt and freshly ground pepper.

Pour this over the goulash before putting in the oven at the beginning of the cooking period.

Eaten without any additional vegetables (or toast or rice !) fish goulash makes an excellent meal for those on a slimming diet.

Trout au Gratin

- *2 trout*
  2 cups white wine
  2 tbs. grated cheese
  4 tbs. breadcrumbs

  2 tbs. butter
  1 small tin mushrooms
  4 tbs. chopped parsley
  salt and pepper

Wash and clean the trout and brush with warmed butter. Place in the soaked RÖMERTOPF and pour on the white wine. Then add the sliced mushrooms and the parsley. Mix the breadcrumbs and the grated cheese and sprinkle this in a layer on the top. Season with salt and pepper and finally add small pieces of butter all over the top. Cover and cook for ¾ hour in a hot oven (400 F. - Gas mark 6). Then remove the lid from the pot and allow to cook for a little longer until the dish is nicely browned on top.

Serve with fresh French bread and salad.

Not suitable for slimmers !

Hungarian Carp

- *1 carp*
  1 glass red wine
  2 cups sour cream
  1 tbs. pork fat

  2 large onions
  4 tbs. tomato puree
  1 lemon
  salt

Clean the carp, then cut into large pieces and remove the larger bones. Sprinkle with salt and paprika pepper. Place the fish in the soaked RÖMERTOPF. Then prepare the sauce separately as follows. Cut the onions into rings and brown them in the hot pork fat in a frying pan. Pour on the red wine and then slowly stir in the sour cream, tomato puree, a little salt and the grated rind of the lemon. Pour this sauce over the fish, then cover and cook in a hot oven (400 F. - Gas mark 6) for about ¾ hour. Before serving season with lemon juice.

Best served with boiled potatoes and endive salad.

Not suitable for slimmers !

Eel Bourguignon

● 1 lb. eel   1 pint red wine
  1 tbs. butter   1 tbs. flour
  2 tbs. chopped parsley   1 tbs. mixed herbs
  a few peppercorns   1 small glass brandy
  2 cloves of garlic   3 onions
  1 tbs. mushrooms

Slice the onions and place them, together with the crushed garlic, the mixed herbs and the peppercorns, in a layer in the bottom of the soaked RÖMERTOPF. Cut the eel into pieces about 3 inches long and place them in the pot. Add a little salt and then pour on the wine and brandy. Cover and cook in a hot oven (425 F. - Gas mark 7) for 40 minutes. Then remove the pieces of eel very carefully and put them on one side. Warm the butter and beat the flour into it and use this to thicken the sauce in the pot. Then replace the eel in the sauce and sprinkle with chopped parsley.

Serve with rice or boiled noodles with butter.

Eel is very fat and not suitable for anyone on a strict slimming diet !

For non-slimmers, however, here is another delicious eel recipe to try out :

Eel in Dill Sauce

- 1½ lb. eel (boned)
  ½ cup stock
  1 lemon
  salt
  1 tbs. dill

  ½ cup white wine
  1 onion
  a little sugar
  freshly ground pepper
  1 cup sour cream

Season the fish with salt and lemon juice and place in the soaked RÖMERTOPF. Pour on the stock and wine and add salt, pepper and sugar. Chop the onion very fine and sprinkle this on top. Cover and cook in a hot oven (425 F. - Gas mark 7) for 40 minutes. Then stir the dill and sour cream carefully into the liquid in the pot.

Serve with potatoes and fresh salad

Fish with Cauliflower

- 1½ lb. fish (filleted)
  2 tbs. butter
  ½ cup grated cheese
  2 tbs. chopped almonds
  salt

  1 large or 2 small
    cauliflowers
  2 tbs. lemon juice
  ½ cup flour
  a little sugar

Divide the cauliflower into smallish pieces and boil in salted water until tender. Put into the soaked RÖMERTOPF alternate layers of cauliflower and fish with small pieces of butter spread in between. Mix together ¼ cup of the water in which the cauliflower has been boiled with a little sugar and salt and the lemon juice. Pour this over the fish and cauliflower. Mix together the cheese, flour and almonds and spread this on top. Cook in a hot oven (425 F. - Gas mark 7) for 45 minutes.

Serve with boiled or mashed potatoes.

French Cod

- 1½ lb. cod (filleted)
  3 tbs. butter

  1 lemon
  1 tbs. flour

½ cup breadcrumbs *mixed French variety)*
1 onion *1 cup white wine*
1 tbs. mixed herbs *salt and pepper*
  (best of all a ready

Cut one tbs. of the butter into small pieces and spread these in the bottom of the soaked RÖMERTOPF. Mix together the chopped onion, the herbs, the lemon juice and half the wine and pour this into the RÖMERTOPF. Place the fish, which has been cut into medium-sized pieces, on this mixture. Cover and cook in a hot oven (400 F. - Gas mark 6) for 40 minutes. Then add the rest of the wine and season with salt and pepper. Thicken the liquid with the flour. Knead the breadcrumbs and butter together and place in pieces on the top of the fish. Replace the pot in the oven without its lid to allow the dish to brown.

Delicious served with French fried potatoes.

Slimmers should take care to eat the fish and not the crust ; then this dish is O.K.

● There are several possible **variations** to this dish :
- use grated cheese instead of breadcrumbs for the crust ;
- mix a few stoned and halved olives into the sauce ;
- prepare the sauce with sour cream instead of with white wine ;
- season with lots of crushed garlic ;
- add 2 finely chopped sweet peppers to the sauce.

Chinese Steamed Fish

● *2 lb. fish (any fish suitable for steaming and boiling will do. It should be boned)*
  ½ lb. leeks *4 oz. bamboo shoots*
  4 oz. mushrooms *4 oz. cooked ham*
  ½ tbs. ground ginger *1 tbs. soy sauce*
  1 cup stock *2 tbs. lemon juice*
  1 tbs. cornflour *1 tbs. brandy*
  a few mixed herbs

Clean the fish, sprinkle with lemon juice and leave for some time to allow the juice to soak well in. Then add a little salt and place in the soaked RÖMERTOPF. Slice the leeks and mushrooms, cut up the ham and bamboo shoots and add these to the fish. Stir the cornflour and brandy into the stock ; season with ground ginger, add the herbs and pour into the Roman Pot. Cover and cook in a hot oven (425 F. - Gas mark 7) for 1¼ - 1½ hours.

Serve with rice.

For a change garnish the dish with shrimps or prawns which have been quickly fried in hot oil.

Excellent for slimmers (without rice !)

Indonesian Fish Casserole

● 1 lb. fish fillets
  4 oz. finely chopped
    almonds
  1 clove of garlic
  soy sauce to taste
  4 tbs. oil

  salt
  1 small tin bamboo shoots
  4 eggs
  salt and pepper
  tabasco to taste
  1 onion

Brush out the soaked RÖMERTOPF with oil. Cut the fish into thin slices and place one layer in the RÖMERTOPF. On top of this layer add the bamboo shoots. Mix the eggs, the finely chopped onion and the almonds together and season this according to taste with soy sauce and tabasco (the original Indonesian fish casserole is very hot !) Pour half this mixture over the fish and bamboo shoots in the Roman Pot. Then add three more layers in the same way : fish, bamboo shoots, liquid. One more thin layer of fish on top. Brush this top layer of fish with oil, cover and cook in a medium oven (375 F. - Gas mark 5) for one hour.

Tuna Fish Casserole

● 1½ tins tuna fish
  3 eggs

  1 sweet pepper
  1 tbs. chopped parsley

salt and pepper	*1 tin mushrooms*
3 cups boiled noodles	*1 tbs. lemon juice*
½ pint cream	

Mix all the ingredients together well, place in the soaked RÖMERTOPF, cover and cook in a moderate oven (350 F. - Gas mark 4) for 1½ hours.

Serve with fresh green salad. Nothing could be simpler — or more delicious !

● Here are a few suggestions for **variations** :
- use rice instead of noodles and add a little tomato puree for added flavour ;
- omit the mushrooms and season with plenty of crushed garlic. Add more chopped parsley ;
  use sliced potatoes instead of noodles, plus about 6 oz. butter ;
- add a dash of cognac.

Small helpings are permitted for slimmers !

Fish Risotto

● *1.lb. fish (filleted)*	*12 oz. rice*
1 tbs. oil	*1 onion*
1 cup grated cheese	*12 oz. tomatoes*
2 pints fish-flavoured stock	

Clean the fish, sprinkle with lemon juice and leave to soak in whilst the rice is prepared. Fry the (washed !) rice and chopped onion for a short time in a frying pan — when the onion turns transparent it is ready. Then transfer to the soaked RÖMERTOPF, together with the stock. Cover and cook in a slow oven (300 F. - Gas mark 1-2) for half an hour. Then remove from the oven and carefully stir in the cheese. Spoon out about half the rice mixture, fill the fish in and put the rice back on top. Skin and halve the tomatoes, then arrange them on top of the rice. Cover and cook in a hot oven (400 F. - Gas mark 6) for a further 20 minutes.

For a special finishing touch garnish each portion with a few shrimps or prawns.

Swiss Fish Casserole

- 1½ lb. cleaned fish
  1 lemon
  2 tbs. chopped parsley
  1 tbs. butter
  1 tbs. flour

  ½ lb. tomatoes
  ½ lb. onions
  1 cup grated cheese
  1 cup sour cream
  salt and pepper

Heat the butter in a frying pan and quickly brown the fish in it. Then put a layer of fish in the bottom of the soaked RÖMERTOPF and sprinkle on half the lemon juice. Skin and slice the tomatoes and chop the onions. Then carefully mix them with the chopped parsley, the grated cheese, seasoning with a little freshly ground pepper. Spread this mixture on top of the first layer of fish. Put another layer of fish on top and sprinkle with the remaining lemon juice. Cover and cook in a hot oven (400 F. - Gas mark 6) for 45 minutes. Then remove from the oven, stir the flour into the sour cream and pour this over the fish. Replace in the oven without the lid and cook until the fish is nicely browned on top.

Best served with French fried potatoes or with rice.

For a change a layer of sliced onions can be added before the final layer of fish.

Swedish Pike with Anchovy

Pike is not a very common dish nowadays, but if you are lucky enough to have one, try the following recipe.

- 1 pike
  2 tbs. butter
  2 tsp. anchovy paste

  1 cup cream
  3 tbs finely chopped
    parsley

Clean the pike and lard it (or wrap it in thin slices of smoked bacon before cooking). Mix the butter and anchovy paste together and spread this thickly inside the pike. Place the pike in the soaked RÖMERTOPF, pour on the cream and sprinkle with the parsley. Cover and cook in a hot oven (400 F. - Gas mark 6) for one hour.

Garnish with slices of lemon and serve with boiled potatoes.

Excellent for slimmers if served with salad instead of potatoes.

Fish with Sauerkraut

- *1 lb. fish (cleaned and*
  boned)
  1 apple
  2 tbs. oil
  ½ pint sour cream
  1 egg

  3 juniper berries
  1 tin sauerkraut
  2 tbs. butter
  4 tbs. flour
  ½ bay leaf
  salt and pepper

Peel, core and slice the apple. Then mix carefully the sauerkraut with the apple, juniper berries and bay leaf and place these ingredients in the soaked RÖMERTOPF. Add 2 tbs. of the sour cream. Cut the fish into fairly large pieces and sprinkle with a little lemon juice. Then dip them in the beaten egg, roll them in flour and quickly brown in hot butter in a frying pan. Then transfer them to the RÖMERTOPF, arranging them carefully on top of the sauerkraut-mixture. Cover and cook in a hot oven (400 F. - Gas mark 6) for one hour. The varying flavours of the dish will now be delightfully combined. For the final touch of perfection : stir one tablespoon of flour into the rest of the sour cream and pour this over the fish. Return to the oven without the lid to allow a golden brown crust to form.

Serve with boiled or mashed potatoes.

Weight-watchers should use yoghurt instead of cream and, instead of frying the fish first, should place it raw on top of the sauerkraut.

● Here are a few suggestions for **varying** the recipe a little :
- prepare the sauce with white wine or cider instead of with sour cream ;
- add 2 chopped sweet peppers to the sauerkraut mixture ;
- chop and fry 4 oz. of bacon and scatter this over the finished dish ;
- add 3-4 peeled and sliced tomatoes at the beginning ;
- before returning the fish to the oven to brown cover with a layer of grated cheese and breadcrumbs (about half a cup of each will be sufficient).

Smoked Fish Casserole

● 1 lb. smoked fish fillets   2 tbs. butter
  1 lb. tomatoes   pepper
  ½ lb. streaky bacon   1 onion

Put a layer of thinly sliced bacon in the bottom of the soaked RÖMERTOPF. Then add the fish and sliced tomatoes and onion. Sprinkle on a little pepper and cover with another layer of bacon slices. Cut the butter into small pieces and sprinkle this on top. Cover and cook in a hot oven (400 F. - Gas mark 6) for about ¾ hour.

Serve with potatoes, boiled or mashed.

Fish Copenhagen

● 1½ lb. fish (filleted)   2 tbs. butter
  1 tbs. chopped parsley   ½ lemon
  1 cup grated cheese   1 lb. potatoes
  1 cup white wine   salt and pepper
  1 tbs. flour   a little paprika pepper

Mix the parsley and a little paprika pepper into the butter (it may be warmed to make this easier — but not melted !) Then cut the butter into pieces and scatter these in the bottom of the soaked RÖMERTOPF. Then put in the peeled, sliced potatoes and on them the fish. Add salt and pepper and lemon juice. On top a little more butter. Cover and cook in a hot oven (400 F. - Gas mark 6) for 1 hour. Then thicken the liquid with a little flour. Sprinkle on the grated cheese and return to the oven without the lid to allow to brown.

Nor for slimmers !

● **Variations :**
- use rice instead of the potatoes ;
- add ½ lb. peas ;
- fry 4 oz. chopped bacon and 2 chopped onions until golden brown ; sprinkle these over the fish before serving ;
- add a small tin of mushrooms ;
- sprinkle generously with chopped dill before serving ;
- add sour cream to the liquid in the RÖMERTOPF and serve this as an excellent sauce ;
- garnish the fish with sliced tomatoes ;
- or, an especially attractive garnish : pile a few prawns or shrimps on each portion.

Hamburg Plaice

Here is a recipe from Germany for plaice — it is equally delicious if sole or flounder are used instead.

● *2 lb. cleaned plaice*
1 small tin peas
4 tomatoes
2 tbs. butter
1 tbs. chopped dill
salt
sugar

For the sauce :
2 tbs. butter
2 tbs. flour
1 cup milk
a little grated nutmeg
salt and pepper

Season the plaice with lemon juice and salt and lay them in the soaked RÖMERTOPF. Sprinkle over them the butter — cut into small pieces — plus the peas and the skinned and halved tomatoes. Season with a little sugar and chopped dill. Cover and cook in a hot oven (400 F. - Gas mark 6) for about 1¼ hours. During the last 20 minutes of cooking time you can prepare the sauce. Melt the butter in a saucepan and stir in the flour. Stir over the heat for about 3 minutes — without browning ! Then slowly add the milk, stirring continually, until the mixture thickens. Season with salt, pepper and grated nutmeg. The fish and sauce should then be ready at the same time to be served together.

Serve with boiled potatoes and salad.

Slimmers should eat this dish without the potatoes — and, unfortunately ! — without the delicious sauce.

VEGETABLES AND CEREALS

You can, of course, use your RÖMERTOPF for cooking many things as well as meat and fish. If you are not using the dish for your meat or main dish, why not try cooking vegetables in it? You'll be delighted with the result. The gentle RÖMERTOPF method of cooking ensures that all the vitamins and goodness of fresh vegetables remain intact — and are not simply boiled away, together with most of the flavour, as so often happens. When cooking vegetables in the RÖMERTOPF remember that you will need to add less liquid than you normally do and will also have to cook for a little longer.

Here are a few suggestions for cooking various vegetable dishes; some are intended to be served with a main meat or fish dish, but I have also included a few recipes intended themselves to form the main dish of a meal.

At the end of this section I have also given a few recipes based on rice or pasta — and have here included the basic recipe for soufflés.

Stuffed vegetables can either be served with something else, or are substantial enough to be served with a sauce as a meal in themselves. They are also an excellent stand-by at buffet dinner parties — and can in fact be prepared before and served cold (either without the sauce, or with a warm sauce prepared just before serving).

Stuffed Tomatoes

● *1½ lb. firm tomatoes*
2 onions
1 egg
2 tbs. grated cheese

2 oz. streaky bacon
1 tsp. chopped parsley
2 tbs. breadcrumbs
salt and pepper

Slice the tops off the tomatoes and carefully remove the pulp. Fry the chopped bacon and onion in a little dripping. When slightly browned remove from the frying pan and now mix thoroughly with the cheese, egg, parsley, breadcrumbs and tomato pulp. Fill this mixture into the tomatoes and place them in the soaked RÖMERTOPF. Cover and cook in a hot oven (450 F. - Gas mark 8) for one hour. Drain off the liquid from the RÖMERTOPF (add a little stock to increase the amount, if you think there isn't enough, or if you want rather a lot of sauce). Thicken with a little flour, stir in some sour cream to make it extra delicious and pour it over the tomatoes before serving.

● **Other fillings :**
- mix 4 eggs, a little salt, 1 finely chopped onion, lots of chopped chives and 2 tbs. grated cheese ;
- mix 2 cups grated cheese, 1 egg, 1 glass yoghurt and season with salt and pepper (add a little curry powder, too, if you fancy a slightly hotter taste).

Various other vegetables may be stuffed in the same way. Try these fillings with *Sweet Peppers, Onions, Cucumber, Aubergines* or small *Marrows*.

Red Cabbage

● *1½ lb. red cabbage*
1 tbs. sugar
2 tbs. red-currant jelly
½ onion
½ bay leaf

2 tbs. butter
2 tbs. vinegar
2 oz. smoked bacon
2 cups stock
salt and pepper

Fry the chopped bacon and onion in a little dripping. Wash the cabbage and shred finely. Place in the soaked RÖMERTOPF and spread the bacon and onion on top. Stir the vinegar, red-currant jelly, salt, pepper and bay leaf into the stock and pour over the cabbage. Cover and cook in a hot oven (400 F. - Gas mark 6) for 1¼ hours. Stir in a little butter before serving.

● **Variations :**
- add two sliced baking apples ;
- use apple wine (or cider) instead of stock ;
- season with caraway seeds ;
- add a few skinned, sliced chestnuts.

Not for slimmers !

Portuguese Beans

● *2 lb. French beans*   *4 oz. smoked bacon*
  7 tomatoes   *½ pint stock*
  pinch savory   *1 garlic clove*
  salt and pepper

Skin and cut up the tomatoes and fry in a pan with the chopped bacon. Put into the soaked RÖMERTOPF. Wash and slice the beans and add to the tomatoes and bacon. Stir salt, pepper, crushed garlic and savory into the stock and pour over the vegetables. Cook for two hours in a hot oven (450 F. - Gas mark 8).

Not for slimmers !

Flemish Chicory

● *2 lb. chicory*   *1 lemon*
  2 tbs. butter   *1 cup stock*

Wash the chicory and drain. Then carefully remove the bitter centre part with a knife. Place in the soaked RÖMERTOPF with small pieces of butter. Mix the stock and juice of the lemon, add a little salt and pepper and cook for $\frac{1}{2}$ hour in a hot oven (450 F. - Gas mark 8).

Is especially delicious served with mashed potato and ham.

Anyone on a slimming diet should halve the amount of butter.

Other Chicory Recipes

Prepare the chicory as above and place in the soaked RÖMER-TOPF with 1 cup cream stirred with 1 cup grated cheese.

Or season the sauce with curry powder.

Or scatter chopped ham over the chicory before cooking.

Or remove the cover shortly before the end of the cooking period and allow the chicory to brown a little.

Chicory in Ham

Before cooking roll the chicory in ham. Thicken the juice with grated cheese.

Brussels Sprouts

● *1 lb. sprouts*
2 small onions
¾ cup stock
1 tbs. butter
grated nutmeg

2 tomatoes
2 tbs. sour cream
1 tbs. flour
salt and pepper

Put the cleaned sprouts, the skinned and quartered tomatoes and the sliced onions into the soaked RÖMERTOPF. Grate on lots of nutmeg. Pour on the stock and add the butter in small pieces.

Cook in a hot oven (400 F. - Gas mark 6) for ½ hour. Stir the flour into the cream and blend into the liquid in the pot.

Not for slimmers !

Mushrooms

● 1½ lb. mushrooms
  (or other fungi)
1 onion
1 tbs. flour
½ lemon
1 small glass brandy

1 tomato
1 tbs. butter
½ cup sour cream
1 tbs. chopped parsley
salt and pepper

Wash and slice the mushrooms. Put in the soaked RÖMERTOPF. Add the peeled and quartered tomato and the chopped onion. Stir together the cream, lemon juice, salt, pepper and brandy and pour over the mushrooms. Add the butter in pieces. Cover and cook in a hot oven (400 F. - Gas mark 6) for ¾ hour. Sprinkle with chopped parsley before serving.

● **Variations :**
- fry 2 oz. chopped bacon and add with the mushrooms ;
- add a little sugar to taste ;
- season with lots of grated nutmeg ;
- cover the mushrooms with sliced cheese ;
- fry small slices of liver in butter and stir into the mushrooms before serving.

Baked Mushrooms

● 1 lb. mushrooms
½ cup grated cheese
1 tbs. butter

1 clove garlic
½ cup breadcrumbs
salt and pepper

Slice the mushrooms and place them in the bottom of the soaked RÖMERTOPF. Sprinkle with salt and pepper. Cut the butter into small pieces and add half. Then stir the cheese and breadcrumbs together and spread them over the mushrooms. Sprinkle with the remaining pieces of butter. Cover and cook in a hot oven (400 F. - Gas mark 6) for about one hour. Then remove the lid and allow to cook for a further 10-15 minutes to allow to brown.

A little chopped streaky bacon or chopped onion can be mixed with the mushrooms before putting into the casserole for a variation in flavour.

Or add a very small glass of white wine to the mushrooms.

Vegetable Casserole

● *1½ lb. mixed vegetables* *½ cup sour cream*
 2 onions *2 cups grated cheese*
 3 tbs. butter *salt and pepper*

Clean and slice the vegetables and chop the onion. Put the vegetables into the soaked RÖMERTOPF in layers, adding lots of grated cheese between. Pour over the cream and add butter in small pieces. Cover and cook in a hot oven (400 F. - Gas mark 6) for about an hour (until the vegetables are tender). Remove the lid for the last ten minutes to allow to brown.

Stuffed Cabbage Leaves

● *6 large cabbage leaves* *12 oz. minced meat*
 2 tbs. breadcrumbs *1 egg*
 1 onion *3 tbs. butter*
 ½ cup stock *mace*
 salt and pepper

Pour boiling water over the cabbage leaves to soften. Mix the meat with the soaked and squeezed breadcrumbs, the chopped onion, a pinch of mace, salt and pepper to taste. Place some of the mixture on each leaf and roll up tightly. Place them close together in the soaked RÖMERTOPF. Add a very small amount of stock and scatter a few knobs of butter on top. Cover and cook in a very hot oven (475 F. - Gas mark 9) for just over an hour. The liquid may then be increased by the addition of more stock and thickened with flour and seasoned to taste.

Serve with boiled potatoes.

● **Variations :**
- prepare a cheese and tomato sauce and pour over the leaves before serving ;
- add sour cream to the sauce ;
- mix some chopped mushrooms into the stuffing ;
- peel and halve 1 lb. tomatoes. Sprinkle with a little salt, pepper and sugar and place in the RÖMERTOPF along with the cabbage leaves. After cooking they will be so soft that they can be stirred into the sauce. If tomatoes are added no further liquid will be required.

Aubergine Casserole

● *1 large aubergine*　　　　*3-4 tomatoes*
　1 cup grated cheese　　　*salt and pepper*
　2 tbs. butter

Slice the aubergine thin and place in the bottom of the soaked RÖMERTOPF. Cover with the sliced tomatoes. Season with salt and pepper, cover and cook in a hot oven (400 F. - Gas mark 6) for about an hour. Then remove from the oven and sprinkle on the grated cheese. Scatter small knobs of butter on top. Return to oven without the lid for a further 10 to 15 minutes to allow to brown.

Moussaka

● *2 aubergines*　　　　　*1 lb. minced beef*
　2 onions　　　　　　　*1 tbs. chopped parsley*
　2 tbs. butter　　　　　*1 clove of garlic*
　a little stock　　　　　*1 tbs. tomato puree*

Chop the onions and fry with the garlic for a few minutes in a
frying pan. Then add the meat and herbs and brown on all sides.
Whilst this mixture is cooking, slice the aubergines and then
sauté in hot butter. Place a layer of aubergines in the bottom of
the soaked RÖMERTOPF and over them put the meat mixture.
Sprinkle with salt and pepper and pour on the stock into which
the tomato puree has been stirred. Cover with another layer of
sliced aubergine. Cover and cook in a hot oven (400 F. - Gas
mark 6) for 1½ hours.

● **Variations :**
- add chopped streaky bacon to the minced beef ;
- add other vegetables to the meat mixture — a chopped carrot
and leek, or sliced mushrooms ;
- add sliced tomatoes ;
- very often moussaka is served with a browned crust : either
take the casserole from the oven, sprinkle generously with grated
cheese and then allow it to brown (without lid !) ; or heat
½ oz butter in a pan and stir 2 tbs. flour into it, gradually
add a cup of milk stirring until the liquid is of an even
consistency, then add a beaten egg and pour this over the
casserole mixture about half an hour before it is ready ; allow to
brown during the final ten minutes cooking time ;
- add a layer of sliced potatoes (raw) on top of the aubergines
and allow these to brown during the final 15 minutes cooking ;
- pour on red wine instead of stock.

Mushroom Goulash

I have called this dish mushroom goulash, but in fact you can use
any sort of edible fungi in it — try experimenting with different
ones for a change and mix them. Some of them have the most
delicious flavours. Of course, there are not always many varieties
available, but you can sometimes get chanterelles or ceps. And if
you can't obtain any fresh ones don't hesitate to try out the
packets of dried ones imported from Italy and Germany.

- *1 lb. fungi*
  1 onion
  ½ bay leaf
  1 cup sour cream
  1 tbs. chopped chives

  1 lb. potatoes
  6 oz. bacon
  1 cup white wine
  1 tbs. chopped parsley
  salt and pepper

Chop the bacon and fry for a few minutes on its own in a frying pan. Then add the chopped onion and fry until golden brown. Wash the fungi and slice. Peel, boil and grate the potatoes. Then add the ingredients in the soaked RÖMERTOPF in layers, first fungi, then potatoes, finally bacon and onion. Stir the cream, herbs and other seasonings with the wine and pour this over the ingredients in the pot. Cover and cook in a hot oven (400 F. - Gas mark 6) for 1¼ hours.

The potatoes make this dish unsuitable for slimmers !

Noodle Casserole

- *½ lb. noodles*
  (wide variety best)
  2 oz. grated cheese
  1 small tin mushrooms
  3 tbs. butter
  1 large onion

  6 oz. cooked ham
  2 tbs. chopped parsley
  2 eggs
  1 cup cream
  salt and pepper

Boil the noodles — don't let them become too soft. Put half of them in the bottom of the soaked RÖMERTOPF. Cut the ham into thin strips and spread this over the noodles. Mix together the eggs, cream, grated cheese, finely chopped onion, and parsley and finally the mushrooms. Pour half this mixture over the noodles, then add another layer of noodles and finally the rest of the egg mixture. Scatter a few small pieces of butter on the top. Cover and cook in a very hot oven (475 F. - Gas mark 9) for a good half hour. Then remove the lid and return to the oven for about 15 minutes until a nice brown crust has formed on top.

Serve with green salad.

● **Variations :**
- use leftovers from the roast instead of the ham ;
- add a little tomato puree to the egg mixture ;
- use minced meat instead of ham ; or try half and half ;
- small chopped vegetables (cauliflower — or peas) instead of mushrooms.

No good for weight-watchers !

Potatoes can also be quite easily prepared in your RÖMERTOPF :
Peel the potatoes and place them in the soaked RÖMERTOPF. Sprinkle with salt and pepper and cover with pieces of butter. Cover and cook for 1 hour in a very hot oven (475 F. - Gas mark 9). Done like this the potatoes are much tastier than when simply boiled. An unusually good flavour can be obtained by scattering the potatoes with caraway seeds before cooking — try it for once !

For *mashed potatoes* prepare as above (no caraway seeds though !), but cut the potatoes into quarters and pour over 2 cups milk before cooking. Before serving the potatoes need simply be stirred into the milk. Try adding chopped parsley.

For excellent *baked potatoes* scrub (don't peel) and place in the soaked RÖMERTOPF . Cook in a very hot oven (475 F. - Gas mark 9) for ½-¾ hour (depends on size). Done like this potatoes are delicious served with salt and lots of butter.

And just in case you think potatoes are a bit of a bore, here are a few special recipe suggestions :

Savoy Potatoes

● *2 lb. potatoes*   *4 oz. onions*
 4 oz. Swiss cheese   *2 oz. butter*
 ½ pint stock   *salt and pepper*
 grated nutmeg

Slice the onions and fry in hot fat until golden brown. Cut the raw potatoes and the cheese into thin slices and mix carefully

with the onions. Place in the soaked RÖMERTOPF. Stir salt and
pepper and a little grated nutmeg into the stock and pour over
the vegetables and cheese. Cook in a hot oven (450 F. - Gas
mark 8) for a little over an hour.

If you'd like to make this dish a little more substantial and
serve it alone, add sliced salami or sausage and return to the
oven for a further ten minutes.

Swiss Potatoes

● *12 potatoes*   *3 onions*
1 cup sour cream   *2 tbs. butter*
grated nutmeg   *salt*

The potatoes should be scrubbed and baked in their jackets (see
above). Allow to cool and then peel and shred. Put into the
soaked RÖMERTOPF. Chop the onions and fry them for a few
minutes in the butter, then add to the potatoes. Season the sour
cream with salt and lots of grated nutmeg and pour over the
potatoes and onions. Cook in a very hot oven (475 F. - Gas
mark 9).

And one final idea :

Potato Goulash

● *2 lb. potatoes*   *½ lb. onions*
1 tsp. paprika pepper   *½ tsp. caraway seeds*
½ tsp. marjoram   *2 oz. dripping*
salt   *stock*

Slice the onions and fry until golden brown. Then put into the
soaked RÖMERTOPF. Cut the potatoes into thin slices and add to
the onions with the caraway seeds, paprika, salt and marjoram.
Half cover with stock. Cook in a hot oven for 50 minutes.

Mushroom Pie

● 1 lb. mushrooms
   puff pastry made from
      about 6 oz. flour
      (or 1 packet deep
      frozen puff pastry)
   2 tbs. butter

½ lb. minced meat
2 eggs
2 tbs. chopped parsley
2 onions
salt and pepper

Roll out the pastry so thin that you have enough to line the RÖMERTOPF ans form a cover. Clean and slice the mushrooms and then fry them for a few minutes in hot butter. Then mix together well with the minced meat, chopped onions, the egg-yolks and then season this mixture with parsley and salt and pepper. Beat the egg-whites until they are quite stiff and then carefully fold into the meat and mushroom mixture. Line the soaked RÖMERTOPF with the pastry and then fill with the meat and mushrooms. Put on a cover of pastry (don't forget to cut 2 or 3 small slits in it, to allow steam to escape). Cover and cook in a hot oven (400 F. - Gas mark 6) for one hour.

The pie should be cut into slices to serve — and is equally delicious hot or cold.

Not suitable for slimmers !

Lasagne

● ½ lb. macaroni
   4 oz. salami
   3 tbs. chopped nuts
   4 oz. grated cheese
   1 clove of garlic
   3 tbs. raisins
   1 tbs. tomato puree

3 oz. butter
4 oz. minced meat
3 eggs
½ onion
2 tbs. chopped parsley
6 oz. tomatoes
salt and pepper

Mix the minced meat together with one of the eggs, the nuts, raisins, crushed garlic and the finely chopped onion. Season with parsley, salt and pepper. Meanwhile hard boil the other 2 eggs and cook the macaroni until it is fairly soft (don't let it get too soft !). Put about one third of the boiled noodles into the bottom of the soaked RÖMERTOPF. Then slice the boiled eggs fairly thinly and arrange half the slices with half the salami on top of the noodles. Form the meat mixture into little balls and place half of them on top of the noodles and eggs. Skin the tomatoes and then either put them through a mincer or mash them with a fork. Add the tomato puree and, if necessary, a little water — so that the mixture has a thick, but liquid, consistency. Pour half of this tomato sauce over the meat balls. Then repeat all these layers again : noodles, egg slices and salami, meat balls, sauce. Finish with a final layer of noodles and scatter the butter, cut into small pieces on top. Cover and cook in a very hot oven (475 F. — Gas mark 9) for 40 minutes. Then remove the lid and allow to brown — for about ten minutes.

Serve with fresh salad.

No variations could make this excellent Roman recipe for lasagne any better !

Completely unsuitable for anyone watching his weight !

Macaroni and Cheese Casserole

● *4 oz. macaroni*   *4 oz. grated cheese*
  4 oz. streaky bacon   *4 eggs*
  ½ pint stock   *2 tbs. butter*
  3 tbs. flour   *freshly ground pepper*
  1 tbs. breadcrumbs

Boil the macaroni until tender, but not too soft. Hard boil the eggs. Melt the butter in a saucepan, stir in the flour and cook for a few moments. Gradually add the stock and cook until an even consistency is obtained. Then reduce the heat and stir in the cheese slowly — stirring all the time to prevent lumps forming. Place half the macaroni in the bottom of the soaked RÖMERTOPF, then pour on the sauce. Chop the bacon and halve the eggs and arrange these on top of the layer of macaroni. Pour on the rest of the sauce. Cover and cook in a hot oven (400 F. -

Gas mark 6) for about half an hour. Then remove the lid, sprinkle on the breadcrumbs and return to the oven for a further ten minutes or so, until the top is nicely browned.

Not suitable for weight-watchers !

Macaroni and Cheese with Cauliflower

- 4 oz. macaroni
  ½ lb. cauliflower
  2 tbs. butter
  ½ pint milk

  4 oz. grated cheese
  3 tbs. flour
  salt and pepper
  1 egg

Boil the macaroni until tender but not too soft. Then carefully stir the grated cheese into it. Put a layer of cauliflower (divided into fairly small sprigs) into the bottom of the soaked RÖMER-TOPF ; then cover with a layer of macaroni and cheese. Continue adding layers until all the ingredients are used up — finishing with macaroni and cheese. Season with salt and pepper. Melt the butter in a saucepan and stir in the flour. Continue to heat for a few moments and then pour in the milk slowly, stirring continually. Boil for 2-3 minutes until the liquid thickens and develops an even consistency. Then remove from the heat and add the egg. Pour this over the ingredients in the RÖMERTOPF. Cover and cook for about ½ hour in a hot oven. Then remove the lid and allow to cook for a further 10-15 minutes to allow to brown.

Not suitable for slimmers !

RICE

Rice must be cooked through without being mushy. Most cooks have their recipes for achieving this — and here is ours for the RÖMERTOPF.

Before cooking the rice wash it well in a strainer under running cold water. This will remove much of the loose starch which makes the grains stick together.

Basic recipe

- 3 cups rice   4½ cups stock
  2 tbs. chopped parsley   ½ tsp. curry powder
  1 tbs. butter

Put the rice with the stock into the soaked RÖMERTOPF. Cook in a hot oven (450 F. - Gas mark 8) for 40 minutes. Then remove the cover and return the rice to the oven for a further ten minutes to allow it to dry a little. Stir in the butter and parsley before serving.

Rice with Onion

Heat one chopped onion in a frying pan. Add the rice and fry for a few minutes until it begins to become transparent. Pour on the stock and season. Bring to the boil and allow to simmer for about five minutes. Put into the soaked, slightly warmed RÖMERTOPF. A further 30 minutes with the cover and 10 without are sufficient to finish the rice to perfection.

Rice with Mushrooms

Heat ½ lb. chopped mushrooms with the rice, following either of the above recipes.

Rice with Peas

Stir 1 small tin of peas into the rice before cooking.

Slimming : anyone on a diet should prepare the rice without salt and fat — and should eat only very limited quantities.

Risotto

- ½ lb. rice   2 pints stock
  1 onion   ½ lb. minced meat
  1 cup grated cheese   ½ lb. tomatoes
  salt and pepper

Wash the rice and then fry briefly in hot fat together with the onions. Then transfer to the soaked RÖMERTOPF together with the stock. Cover and cook for about half an hour in a moderate oven (300 F. - Gas mark 1-2). Then remove from the oven and stir the grated cheese into the rice. Then carefully lift out the top half of the rice with a spoon and put in the minced meat. Fill back the rice, arrange the skinned tomatoes on top and return to the oven. Cover and cook for a further 20 minutes in a hot oven (400 F. - Gas mark 6).

● Here are some of our suggestions for **variations** to this (there is also a recipe for fish risotto on page 86) :
- chop 6 oz. bacon up and fry in a pan. After a few moments add the chopped onion and rice and fry until golden brown. Replace some of the liquid by thinned tomato puree ;
- add ½ lb. of finely sliced sweet peppers to the rice in the RÖMERTOPF. Season with paprika pepper ;
- use chicken liver instead of minced meat ; add chopped mushrooms to the rice ;
- use sliced salami instead of the minced meat and season with sage and rosemary ; garnish with anchovies ;
- risotto is an ideal dish for using up leftovers. Almost all kinds of meat and vegetable can be incorporated into it. Adapt our basic recipe to suit the ingredients you have to hand !

Not suitable for slimmers.

Here is just one more special recipe for risotto :

Mushroom Risotto

- 12 oz. rice
  4 oz. butter
  3 oz. asparagus spears
  3 oz. parmesan cheese
  1 cup white wine
  ½ onion
  3 oz. ham
  3 oz. mushrooms (or try

  other fungi for a change
  — chanterelles or the
  dried mixed fungi
  from Italy)
  1 pint stock
  ½ cup cream
  2 tomatoes

Chop the mushroom and fry with the rice in a pan until turning pale brown. Then add the fungi, asparagus, the chopped ham, the peeled and chopped tomatoes and allow to cook gently for a few minutes. Then transfer everything to the soaked RÖMERTOPF. Pour on the stock and the white wine and season with salt, pepper and a little savory. Cover and cook in a hot oven (425 F. - Gas mark 7) for about 40 minutes. Before serving stir in the grated cheese, the remaining butter and the slightly warmed cream.

Not for slimmers !

BREAD

The RÖMERTOPF is excellent for warming up white bread which has lost its original crispness. If you have ever bought French bread for dinner or fresh breakfast rolls and then discovered that, only a few hours later, they have already lost their crispness, then you have no doubt popped them into the oven and warmed them up a little. This is a method which is only half successful — it makes the outside crisp, but inside the bread is still cold and no longer so fresh. Try putting them into the RÖMERTOPF and the bread will be fresh right the way through.

Put the rolls (cut a French loaf into two pieces so that it fits in !) into the RÖMERTOPF — which, for once, has *not been*

soaked in water. Put a few tiny knobs of butter on the crust.
Put on the cover and place in the cold oven. Then switch on to
475 F. - Gas Mark 9) and leave for fifteen minutes. The bread
will be warmed right through. In order to get a nice crispy
crust, switch off the oven and leave for a further ten minutes.
That's all !

One very satisfied RÖMERTOPF customer in Germany wrote and
told us that she even used her RÖMERTOPF for baking bread ! I
haven't tried this yet — but you see how versatile the dish can
be !

SOUFFLES

● *5 tbs. butter*   *4 eggs*
  1 cup warmed milk   *½ cup flour*
  pinch of salt

Warm the butter in a saucepan and stir in the flour. Cook for
about three minutes, without browning. Then gradually add the
milk and bring to the boil. Allow to boil for about one minute,
stirring continually to prevent any lumps forming. The liquid
should thicken slowly. When you have a nice even consistency,
add the egg-yolks. Beat the egg-whites until quite stiff and then
fold in carefully. Grease the soaked RÖMERTOPF with some more
butter and pour in the egg mixture. Cover and cook in a hot
oven (400 F. - Gas mark 6) for almost an hour.

This is the basic recipe for soufflés cooked in the RÖMERTOPF.
But soufflés are, of course, most delicious when flavoured with
some additional ingredient. The flavouring should be added
after you have stirred in the egg-yolks. The soufflé may either
be sweet (and we have included a few recipes for sweet soufflés
in our section on desserts — see p. 127, 128) or savouries. Our
favourite savoury soufflé is made with cheese and here is our
recipe for it.

Cheese Soufflé

- 3 oz. butter
  3 oz. flour
  ½ pint milk
  2 tbs. finely chopped
  parsley

  4 eggs
  2 cups grated cheese
  a little grated nutmeg
  salt and pepper

Prepare sauce from flour, butter and milk as described above. Then remove from the heat and carefully stir in the egg-yolks and the grated cheese. Season with a little grated nutmeg and salt and pepper. Then beat the egg-whites until quite stiff and carefully fold in. Grease the soaked RÖMERTOPF with some more butter and pour in the egg mixture. Cover and cook in a hot oven (400 F. - Gas mark 6) for 55 minutes.

Serve with fresh salad.

Not suitable as part of a slimming diet.

SOUPS

The RÖMERTOPF is a real treasure when soup is on the menu. It's an age-old rule that the longer a soup cooks the better it becomes, for then the flavours of vegetables and meat really blend with the liquid. And in the RÖMERTOPF there is no danger at all of ingredients sticking or being burned, or of the liquid gradually boiling away. The aroma and full flavour of all the ingredients are enclosed in the casserole, so that truly excellent soups are the result. And it is so easy !

The following are just a few suggestions which are bound to give you lots of new ideas.

Mushroom Soup

- *1 lb. mushrooms*
  3 oz. butter
  1½ pints chicken stock
  ½ onion

  ½ cup cream
  juice of ½ lemon
  grated nutmeg
  salt and pepper

Wash and chop the mushrooms. Fry the chopped onions in a little hot fat and add the mushrooms for 2-3 minutes. Then transfer to the soaked RÖMERTOPF and pour on the stock. Add the lemon juice, salt and pepper and small pieces of butter. Close and cook in a hot oven (400 F. - Gas mark 6) for at least an hour. Stir in the cream before serving, and grate on a little nutmeg.

As an alternative to nutmeg chopped parsley may be sprinkled on the soup before serving.

French Onion Soup

● 1 lb. onions
2 tbs. butter
2 pints stock
4 slices white bread

2 cups grated cheese
pinch sugar
pinch curry powder

Chop the onions finely and fry until golden brown. Pour the stock into the soaked RÖMERTOPF and add the onions. Sprinkle with curry powder and sugar. Cover and cook in a hot oven (400 F. - Gas mark 6) for at least 1¼ hours. Then remove the lid carefully, place the bread in the soup and sprinkle with the grated cheese. Put back into the oven without the lid and cook for a few more minutes, until golden brown on top.

The bread will be delightfully crisp on top if toasted before being put into the soup.

As an alternative seasoning add a few drops of vinegar and a crushed clove of garlic.

And one especially fine alternative : use 1½ pints stock and ½ pint white wine.

This delicious recipe is unfortunately not suitable for slimmers.

Mixed Vegetable Soup

● 1½ lb. vegetables
2 pints stock

4 tbs. grated cheese
salt and pepper

Clean and cut up the vegetables. Fry quickly in a little hot fat. Then transfer to the soaked RÖMERTOPF together with the stock and salt and pepper to taste. Cover and cook in a hot oven (400 F. - Gas mark 6) for about 1½ hours (until the vegetables are tender, but not mushy). Sprinkle with grated cheese before serving.

Chinese Vegetable Soup

- ½ lb. pork
  4 oz. bamboo shoots
  2 oz. mushrooms
  ½ onion
  1 oz. Chinese glass noodles
  2 pints chicken stock

  1 tbs. soyabean sauce
  1 tbs. vinegar
  1 tbs. cornflour
  1 tbs. butter
  a little sugar
  salt and pepper

Cut the meat into thin slices and fry for a few minutes in hot butter. Transfer to the soaked RÖMERTOPF, together with the finely sliced onions, chopped mushrooms and the bamboo shoots. Stir the soyabean sauce, vinegar, sugar, salt and pepper into the stock and pour over the meat. Add the cornflour and noodles. Cook in a hot oven (450 F. - Gas mark 8) for at least an hour. The soup should be smooth and creamy. Cook for a little longer if it is too thin.

Special Pea Soup
(just to prove that pea soup does not have to be dull !)

- ½ lb. dried peas
  ½ lb. boiled ham
  3 potatoes

  bouquet garni
  ½ pint white wine
  1½ pints stock

Soak the peas overnight. Then put into the soaked RÖMERTOPF with the chopped ham, stock, white wine, chopped potatoes and bouquet garni. Cook in a hot oven (400 F. - Gas mark 6) for at least 2½ hours. Sprinkle with chopped parsley before serving.

For variation the soup can be seasoned with marjoram, or with crushed garlic, or with thyme and pepper, and served with croutons.

Not for slimmers !

Ox-tail Soup

- 1½ lb. ox-tail
  2 oz. smoked bacon

  1 onion
  bouquet garni

2 pints stock

1 cup boiled rice

1 tbs. cornflour

1 tsp. lemon juice

½ pint sour cream

½ cup sweet wine

a little thyme

sugar

lemon juice

Joint the ox-tail. Cut the bacon into pieces and fry. Then add the ox-tail to the frying pan for a few minutes, plus the onion. Transfer to the soaked RÖMERTOPF and pour on the stock. Add salt, pepper, thyme and a little sugar. Cook in a moderate oven (350 F. - Gas mark 4) for 3 hours. Then strain the soup through a sieve. Thicken the liquid with the cornflour and add the wine and lemon juice. Beat the cream briefly and stir into the soup. Finally cut the meat from the ox-tail and add to the soup, together with the rice.

A good dish for slimmers !

● **Variations :**
- add more rice and then don't thicken with cornflour ;
- add chopped mushrooms at the beginning ;
- add a few skinned and quartered tomatoes ;
- sprinkle each portion with chopped, fried bacon.

Potato Soup

● 2 lb. potatoes   1 onion
  ½ lb. minced meat   bouquet garni
  2 pints stock   marjoram
  2 tbs. chopped bacon   salt and pepper
  2 tbs. butter

Fry the bacon and chopped onion, then add the meat and fry until browned. Transfer to the soaked RÖMERTOPF, plus the bouquet garni and the peeled, chopped potatoes. Pour in the stock and season with marjoram. Cover and cook in a hot oven (400 F. - Gas mark 6) for 1¼ hours. Add salt and pepper to taste. Add a knob of butter to each portion before serving.

Not suitable for slimmers !

● The seasonings can be **varied** in several ways :
- add lots of caraway seeds ;
- use thyme and crushed garlic instead of marjoram.
- or, add chopped sausage and/or mushrooms, and, as an especially fine finishing touch — stir in cream before serving.

Pot-au-Feu

- ● ¾ lb. meat
  ¾ lb. chicken pieces
  ½ lb. carrots
  ½ cup grated cheese
  ½ cup white wine
  bouquet garni

  4 oz. noodles
  1 garlic clove
  1½ pints stock
  sugar
  salt and pepper

Cut the meat into cubes and place in the soaked RÖMERTOPF with the stock and bouquet garni. Cook in a hot oven (400 F. - Gas mark 6) for about 2 hours. Add the chopped carrots and cook for a further hour. Boil the noodles until soft and add to the soup before serving. Season with a little sugar, crushed garlic, salt, pepper, wine and grated cheese.

Can be served with slices of toast as a main dish.

Suitable for slimmers if the noodles are omitted.

● **As a variation** the soup can be seasoned with thyme, cloves and a bay leaf ;
- or sprinkled with chopped parsley before serving ;
- or the wine replaced by a glass of cognac ;
- or 2 oz. chopped bacon added before serving.

Fish Chowder

● ½ lb. fish
  3 potatoes
  2-3 carrots
  1 onion
  1 pint fish stock

  ¼ pint milk
  1 tbs. butter
  parsley
  salt and pepper

Bone and skin the fish, peel and chop the potatoes and carrots. Chop the onion and fry until transparent. Put the stock and vegetables into the soaked RÖMERTOPF. Cover and cook for about 1 hour in a hot oven (400 F. - Gas mark 6). Then add the fish and milk and replace in the oven for a further ½ hour. Season to taste. Sprinkle with parsley before serving.

Another really excellent soup is the fish soup which is prepared with many different sorts of fish in the Mediterranean countries. Here is a French version :

Bouillabaisse

● 1½ lbs. fish fillets
  3 tbs. shrimps
  a few mussels
  1 onion
  2 tbs. oil
  bouquet garni
  1 bay leaf
  salt and pepper

  2 tomatoes
  a little grated lemon
    rind
  2 pints stock
  2 tbs. butter
  ½ lb. potatoes
  2 tbs. brandy
  pinch saffron

The fish may be of any obtainable sorts — but should be as mixed and varied as possible.

Heat the oil and fry the chopped onions and crushed garlic in it. Tear the fish into pieces and add to the frying pan for a few minutes. Grease the soaked RÖMERTOPF with butter and then place a few small pieces of butter in the bottom. Peel and cut up the potatoes and tomatoes and place in the RÖMERTOPF. Add the fish. Stir the saffron, bay leaf, lemon rind, salt and pepper into the stock and pour over the fish and vegetables. Cook in a hot oven (400 F. - Gas mark 6) for one hour. Taste and season again if necessary. Pour in the brandy. Add a few shrimps and mussels to each portion before serving.

Can be served with toast.

Slimmers cut down the amounts of oil and butter.

And to finish off this chapter, two famous and really fine Slav soups :

Bortsch

- *2½ pints good quality beef stock*
- *4 large beetroot (uncooked)*
- *salt and pepper*

The stock should be made from meat and not just cubes and ideally ought to have a little shredded beef in it.

Put the stock into the soaked RÖMERTOPF. Clean the beetroot, shred and add to the stock. Cover and cook in a hot oven (375 F. - Gas mark 5) for at least an hour (until the beetroot is cooked). Strain to remove the beetroot and season with salt and pepper. A little lemon juice may also be added.

Serve with beef patties.

The soup may be enriched by the addition of finely sliced beef before serving.

Serbian Bean Soup

- ½ lb. white beans
  4 tbs. fat
  2 tomatoes
  ½ tbs. paprika pepper
  2 tbs. chopped parsley
  salt and pepper

  4 oz. cooked ham
  2 large onions
  2 tbs. tomato puree
  2 potatoes
  mixed herbs (thyme,
     marjoram, rosemary)

Soak the beans overnight. Put them with the water in which they have been soaking into the soaked RÖMERTOPF. Cut the ham into strips, chop the onions, peel and cut up the tomatoes and potatoes and add all these to the beans. Stir in the tomato puree, herbs, salt and pepper. Cook in a hot oven (450 F. - Gas mark 8) for 1½ hours. The soup should be very thick. Sprinkle with chopped parsley before serving.

A cup of rice may be added in place of the potatoes.

The soup may also be thickly sprinkled with grated cheese before serving.

Not suitable for anyone on a slimming diet !

THE "SWEET" RÖMERTOPF: DESSERTS AND JAMS

The RÖMERTOPF is also excellent for preparing sweet dishes. This does mean buying an additional RÖMERTOPF, but after you have used it once or twice you will be convinced that this little extra outlay was well worth it. Never be tempted to cook meat or fish in your "sweet" RÖMERTOPF (or vice versa!) — otherwise you will spoil that fragrance of fruit, sugar and vanilla which is a special part of it.

Baked Apples

- 8 medium-sized apples
  4 tbs. sugar
  4 tbs. chopped almonds
  4 tbs. raisins

  1 tbs. butter
  1 tbs. rum
  pinch cinnamon
  ½ cup wine

Do not peel the apples, but carefully remove the cores. Mix together the sugar, almonds, raisins, rum and cinnamon. A little cream may also be added, if desired, to make the mixture especially fine and smooth. Fill this mixture into the apples and stand them in the bottom of the soaked RÖMERTOPF. Pour the wine over them and add the butter in small pieces. Cover. Cook in a very hot oven (475 F. - Gas mark 9) for about half an hour. The cooking time required will depend very much on the sort of apples you use — after half an hour some will already be quite soft, whilst others are still too hard.

The apples may alternatively be peeled. This is in fact a good idea if you are going to serve them with a sauce — one delicious idea is to pour advocaat over them.

● The filling can be **varied** in many ways :
- simply fill with jam ;
- use honey in place of sugar ;
- add chopped pineapple to the mixture ;
- stuff with dates ;
- add a little grated orange rind and orange juice.

And two more delectable suggestions : instead of pouring wine over the apples, use cream into which a few drops of vanilla essence have been stirred ; or stick the apples all over with splinters of almond before cooking.

Stewed Apples

● *4 lb. apples*
1 lb. sugar
½ tsp. cinnamon

Peel, core and slice the apples. Place in the soaked RÖMERTOPF with the sugar and cinnamon. Add a little water to cover the bottom of the pot. Cover and cook in a hot oven (400 F. - Gas mark 6) until the fruit is tender (about ¾ hour).
Serve with fresh cream or custard.

Pears, plums, apricots, damsons, etc., may also be stewed in the same way. More water should be added for very dry fruits, such as hard pears — which will also take longer to cook. More sugar should be added to sour fruit.

For a change try stewing different fruits mixed — apples and brambles, oranges and prunes, apricots and apples. Think up your own combinations — some of the most unusual mixtures are the most delicious !

Apple Pie

- *Short or flaky pastry
  from 8 oz. flour
  2½ lb. cooking apples*

*6 oz. sugar
few drops lemon juice
2-3 cloves*

Line the soaked RÖMERTOPF with half the pastry. Peel and core the apples and cut into slices. Place them with the sugar and cloves in the pastry lining. Add the lemon juice. Make a cover for the pie with the remaining pastry, not forgetting to pierce a few holes in it. Cover and cook in a hot oven (400 F. - Gas mark 6) for just over an hour. Then remove the lid and cook for a further 10-15 minutes to allow the crust to brown.

● **Variations :**

- soft fruit such as brambles mixed with the apples gives a particularly juicy pie ;
- a little ground ginger may also be used to flavour the apple ;
- try soaking 3 tbs. raisins in 2 tbs. rum for a short time and adding these to the apple.

The pie may also be made without the pastry lining. Fill the fruit straight into the soaked RÖMERTOPF and use half the amount of pastry to make a cover for the top.

Apple Crumble

- *2 lb. apples
  6 oz. flour
  4 oz. sugar*

*4 tbs. butter
a little cinnamon
few drops lemon juice*

Peel, core and slice the apples. Put into the soaked RÖMERTOPF and sprinkle with cinnamon and lemon juice. Rub the fat into the flour and sugar until you have a fine mixture, like bread-crumbs. Sprinkle this on top of the fruit. Cover and cook in a moderately hot oven (350 F. - Gas mark 4) for about 1 hour. Then remove the cover ; replace the pot in the oven and cook for a little longer until the crust is brown.

Serve with fresh cream or with custard.
The crumble may be made with other fruits.

Not suitable for slimmers !

Apfelstrudel

● 2 lb. apples
4 oz. chopped nuts
4 oz. sugar
2 oz. raisins
juice and grated rind
   of ½ lemon
few drops vanilla essence
1 cup milk
1 small glass rum
cinnamon

melted butter to brush
  pastry

For the pastry :

½ lb. flour
3 tbs. melted butter
1 egg
3 tbs. water
pinch salt

Knead a dough from the flour, egg, butter, water and salt. Shape into a ball and leave to stand in a warm place for half an hour. Then roll out the dough until very thin (you should be able to see the light through it !). Brush with melted butter. Peel and core the apples and cut into thin slices. Marinade in the rum and lemon juice. Then mix with the sugar, nuts, vanilla essence and grated lemon rind and place on the rolled out dough. Sprinkle with cinnamon. Roll up and cut into two pieces. Place in the soaked RÖMERTOPF. Brush on a little more butter and sprinkle with sugar. Stir a few drops of vanilla essence and a little sugar into the milk and pour carefully into the RÖMERTOPF with the strudel. Cook in a hot oven (400 F. - Gas mark 6) for an hour. Then remove the cover and cook for a little longer to allow a nice brown crust to form.

Not suitable for slimmers !

Strawberry Soufflé

● *1½ cups strawberries*
  ½ cup sugar
  2 tbs. lemon juice
  4 eggs
  1 small glass brandy
  ½ tbs. grated lemon rind

To grease the RÖMERTOPF :

2 tbs. butter
2 tbs. sugar

Grease the soaked RÖMERTOPF thickly with butter and sprinkle with sugar. Put in a warm place. Put the strawberries, lemon juice, lemon rind and sugar in a saucepan and bring slowly to the boil. Remove from the heat and stir in the brandy. Allow to cool for about ten minutes, then add the egg-yolks. Finally fold in the stiffly beaten egg-whites and pour into the RÖMERTOPF. Cover. Cook in a hot oven (400 F. - Gas mark 6) for 40 minutes. Garnish with strawberries and cream.

Not suitable for slimmers !

Rum Soufflé

● *2 oz. chocolate*
  ½ cup sugar
  3 tbs. butter
  2 tbs. flour
  1 cup warm milk
  ½ tsp. vanilla essence
  2 tbs. rum
  4 eggs
  pinch salt

To grease the RÖMERTOPF :

2 tbs. butter
2 tbs. sugar

Grease the soaked RÖMERTOPF thickly with butter and sprinkle with sugar. Melt the chocolate in a basin over hot water. Melt the butter in a small saucepan and stir in the flour and salt. Cook gently for 1-2 minutes. Then gradually stir in the milk and sugar, beating continuously to avoid lumpiness. Stir until it comes to the boil and then continue heating until it is of an even thickness. Remove from the heat, add the vanilla essence and the chocolate and allow to cool for ten minutes. Then stir in the rum and egg-yolks. Carefully fold in the stiffly beaten egg-whites. Pour into the slightly warmed RÖMERTOPF and cook in a hot oven (400 F. - Gas mark 6) for one hour. Serve immediately. As a final finishing touch : garnish each portion with a spoonful of ice-cream.

Not for anyone who wants to lose weight !

Cherry Brandy Soufflé

● *3 tbs. flour*
3 tbs. butter
¾ cup hot milk
½ cup chopped nuts
½ cup sugar
4 eggs
4 tbs. cherry brandy

To grease RÖMERTOPF :

2 tbs. butter
2 tbs. sugar

Grease the soaked RÖMERTOPF thickly with butter and sprinkle with sugar. Melt the butter in a saucepan and add the flour. Stir for 2 minutes. Gradually add the milk, stirring continually. Bring to the boil again and continue to heat until it thickens. Add the sugar. Remove from the heat and allow to cool. Stir in the egg-yolks and cherry brandy. Fold in the stiffly beaten egg-whites. Pour into the RÖMERTOPF and sprinkle with chopped nuts. Cover. Cook in a hot oven (400 F. - Gas mark 6) for 40 minutes.

Not for slimmers !

Bread Pudding

- *1 loaf white bread*   *4 oz. sultanas*
  ¾ pint milk   *3 tbs. sugar*

Cut the bread into slices and soak in the milk. Grease the soaked RÖMERTOPF with butter. Put the sliced bread into the RÖMERTOPF in layers, adding sultanas and a sprinkling of sugar between layers. Finish with bread. Cover and cook in a hot oven (450 F. - Gas mark 8) for 45 minutes. Remove the cover about 5 minutes before the end of the cooking time to allow the top to brown.

This recipe can be varied by adding a layer of fruit at the bottom (apple, plum, etc.).

Not for slimmers !

Bohemian Bread Pudding

- *8 breakfast rolls*   For the sauce :
  ½ pint milk
  4 oz. raisins   *3 eggs*
  6 apples   *½ pint milk*
  2 oz. chopped almonds   *1 tbs. sugar*
  5 tbs. sugar   *vanilla essence*
  1 tbs. cinnamon
  2 tbs. butter

Cut the rolls into thin slices and soak in the warmed milk. Grease the soaked RÖMERTOPF with butter and put in a layer of bread. Peel and grate the apples and mix with the raisins, almonds, sugar and cinnamon. Put a layer of this mixture on top of the bread and continue adding rolls and apple in layers, finishing with rolls. Heat the remaining milk. Beat the eggs and sugar. Pour the milk onto the eggs and sugar and stir well. Add the vanilla essence. Pour this over the apple and rolls in the

RÖMERTOPF. Scatter a few small pieces of butter on the top. Cook for 1 hour in a hot oven (400 F. - Gas mark 6).

Not suitable for anyone interested in staying slim !

Baked Milk Pudding

● 3 tbs. rice (or sago   1½ tbs. sugar
   or tapioca)   ½ tbs. butter
  1 pint milk   grated nutmeg

Put the rice in the soaked RÖMERTOPF with the milk and sugar. Sprinkle with grated nutmeg and add a few small pieces of butter. Cover and cook in a moderate oven (375 F. - Gas mark 5) for about 2½ hours. Then remove the cover and cook for a further ½ hour. The gentle heat in the RÖMERTOPF is ideal for cooking milk puddings — which may also be flavoured with a little vanilla essence, or caramel or chocolate.

Bavarian Sweet Dumplings

● For the Pastry :
  ½ lb. flour   1 oz. yeast
  2 eggs   ½ pint milk
  2 tbs. butter   4 oz. butter
  ½ cup milk   vanilla essence

Mix the ingredients for the pastry together well. Leave for about 1½ hours in a warm place to rise. Soak and warm the RÖMERTOPF a little and put into it the milk and the vanilla essence. Cut the butter into pieces and add to the milk. Divide the pastry into pieces about the size of an egg and drop them into the milk. Cover the RÖMERTOPF with a clean cloth and leave for a further 30 minutes. Then put on the lid and cook for ¾ hour in a very hot oven.

    Serve with vanilla sauce or with custard.

Not suitable for anyone on a slimming diet !

Cherry Pudding
(a recipe from Baden in Southern Germany)

- 5 breakfast rolls
  1 pint milk
  4 oz. butter
  4 oz. sugar
  1 small glass rum
  1 lb. cherries (ideally
    they should be a
    mixture

  of morello and
    sweeter cherries)
  1 cup raisins
  a little cinnamon and
    ground cloves
  a few drops vanilla
    essence
  4 eggs.

Soak the rolls in milk and at the same time allow the raisins to stand for a time in the rum. Beat the butter and sugar and then the eggs with them until light and frothy. Then mix with the rolls, raisins, cinnamon and cloves, the vanilla essence and a small packet of custard powder. Grease the soaked RÖMERTOPF with butter and put in a layer of this mixture. Then put in the cherries and cover them with another layer of the mix. Cover and cook in a hot oven (400 F. - Gas mark 6) for 1 hour.

May be served either hot or cold — most delicious with vanilla sauce.

Not for weight-watchers !

Here is an absolutely delightful recipe for flambé bananas given to me the other day by a musical friend of mine — her enthusiasm for the RÖMERTOPF has its origins somewhere in an admiration for all things Roman ! (She says she practises the piano whilst the food cooks !)*

Bananas Flambé

- 2 lbs. ripe bananas
  (overripe better than
  any tending to be at all
  green)

  4 oz. butter
  4 oz. sugar
  ½ cup brandy

Cut the bananas in half lengthways and lay them in the bottom of the soaked RÖMERTOPF. Cut the butter into pieces and cover the bananas with these and the sugar. Cover and cook in a hot oven (425 F. - Gas mark 7) for 1 hour. Shortly before you take the bananas from the oven warm the brandy. Then take the RÖMERTOPF from the oven, pour on the brandy and light. The brandy should burn for a few moments and leave a delicious flavour in the hot sugared bananas. Serve immediately. The bananas are marvellous served alone, but can also be served with cream and a sweet biscuit.

JAM-MAKING

Yes, you can make jams and marmelades in your sweet RÖMERTOPF. Here again it is of great advantage that nothing can burn or even be slightly caught. You can make delicious full fruit jams. For making large quantities you will need the extra large RÖMERTOPF, but for a start a small one will do. The amounts given in the following recipes are intended for the smaller size — for about 1½ lbs. of fruit.

For a basic recipe you need 1½ lbs. fruit (washed and stoned), ¾ lb. sugar and ½ lb. preserving sugar. Cook in a hot oven (400 F. - Gas mark 6) for 1½ hours.

Now try out some of our special recipes :

Marmelade

● 2 lb. oranges (with peel)   ¼ pint water
1¼ lb. sugar   juice of 1 lemon

Wash the fruit and dry well (if the fruit has been treated with chemicals then be sure to wash very well in hot water). Boil in water for about 15 minutes. Thinly peel half the oranges, and cut the peel into thin strips. Peel remaining fruit, divide into sections, remove the seeds and pith. Cut into pieces. Mix with the strips of rind, the sugar, water and lemon juice. Put into the soaked RÖMERTOPF and cover. Cook in a hot oven (400 F. - Gas mark 6) for 1½ hours. .

Bramble Jam

- 2 lb. brambles
  1¾ lb. sugar
  juice of 1 lemon

Wash the fruit. Mix with the sugar and lemon juice. Put into the soaked RÖMERTOPF and cook in a hot oven (400 F. - Gas mark 6) for about 1½ hours.

Rhubarb and Strawberry Jam

- 1 lb. rhubarb
  ½ lb. strawberries
  1¼ lb. sugar
  1 tsp. ground ginger

  1 cup chopped pineapple
  ½ cup water
  a few drops vanilla essence

Clean the rhubarb and cut into small pieces. Put into the soaked RÖMERTOPF, cover with the sugar and vanilla essence and leave to stand for about an hour. Halve the strawberries and add to the rhubarb, together with the pineapple and ground ginger. Cover and cook in a hot oven (400 F. - Gas mark 6) for about 1½ hours.

Mixed Fruit Jam

- ½ lb. cherries
  (stoned)
  ½ lb. raspberries

  ½ lb. black currants
  (or red currants)
  1¾ lb. sugar

Clean the fruit and put into the soaked RÖMERTOPF with the sugar. Cook for about 1 hour in a hot oven (400 F. - Gas mark 6).

Raspberry Jam

- 1½ lb. raspberries
  1¼ lb. sugar

  1 orange
  pinch cinnamon

Wash the raspberries and put into the soaked RÖMERTOPF with the sugar. Leave to stand for about an hour. Add the cinnamon, the juice and grated rind of the orange. Cover and cook in a hot oven (400 F. - Gas mark 6) for 1½ hours.

Mandarine Jam

- 2 lb. mandarines
  (with peel)
  1¾ lb. sugar

  1 small glass brandy
  1 tsp. small pieces of
  ginger

Peel mandarines and remove seeds. Cut into pieces. Wash half the peel thoroughly in hot water, cut into thin strips and mix with the fruit. Stir in the sugar, ginger and brandy. Put into the soaked RÖMERTOPF, cover, and cook in a hot oven (400 F. - Gas mark 6) for 2 hours. Try this unusual delicious jam for a change.

Plum Jam

- 2 lb. plums
  1¾ lb. sugar

  1 small glass rum ·
  1 lemon

Clean and stone the plums. Cut into small pieces (or put through the mincer). Pour on the juice from the lemon and the rum. Leave to stand for a few hours. Then stir in the sugar, put into the soaked RÖMERTOPF, cover, and cook in a hot oven (400 F. - Gas mark 6) for 1½ hours.

Lemon Marmelade

Make as for marmelade.

Peach and Melon Jam

● *1 lb. peaches (stoned)*   *1¼ lb. sugar*
  ½ lb. melon pieces   *1 lemon*

Cut the peaches into small pieces and the melon into thin strips.
Put into the soaked RÖMERTOPF together with the sugar. Cover
and cook in a hot oven (400 F. - Gas mark 6) for 1½ hours.
Stir the juice and grated rind of a lemon into the mixture whilst
still hot.

Pear and Cranberry Jam

● *1 lb. cranberries*   *1 lemon*
  ½ lb. pears   *vanilla essence*
  1¼ lb. sugar

Wash the cranberries, put into the soaked RÖMERTOPF, add the
sugar and leave to stand for an hour. In the meantime peel and
core the pears and cut into small pieces. Mix with the cranberries. Cover and cook in a hot oven (400 F. - Gas mark 6) for
1½ hours. Whilst still hot stir in the vanilla essence, juice and
grated rind of a lemon.

Cherry Jam

One final recipe for Cherry jam, from the Black Forest. In the
Black Forest they are real geniuses at developing recipes for
cherries (their cherry cake is absolutely delicious !) :

● *1½ lb. cherries*   *2 oz. almonds*
  1¼ lb. sugar   *5 tbs. kirsch*

Wash the cherries, remove the stalks and stones. Mix with the
sugar, put into the soaked RÖMERTOPF and leave to stand
overnight. Cover and cook in a hot oven (400 F. - Gas mark 6)

for 1½ hours. Whilst still hot stir in the lemon juice, chopped almonds and kirsch.

The following pages have been left empty for your own RÖMER-TOPF recipes. We wish you lots of success with your cooking and hope you'll write and tell us if you have any bright ideas of your own !

Eduard BAY.

For your own RÖMERTOPF recipes :

_____

_____

_____

_____

_____

_____

_____

_____

_____

_____

_____

_____

_____

_____

For your own RÖMERTOPF recipes:

For your own RÖMERTOPF recipes :

_____

_____

_____

_____

_____

_____

_____

_____

_____

_____

_____

_____

_____

For your own RÖMERTOPF recipes:

_____

_____

_____

_____

_____

_____

_____

_____

_____

_____

_____

_____

_____

_____

For your own RÖMERTOPF recipes :

_____

_____

_____

_____

_____

_____

_____

_____

_____

_____

_____

_____

_____

_____

For your own RÖMERTOPF recipes :

_____

_____

_____

_____

_____

_____

_____

_____

_____

_____

_____

_____

_____

_____

For your own RÖMERTOPF recipes:

_____

_____

_____

_____

_____

_____

_____

_____

_____

_____

_____

_____

_____

_____

For your own RÖMERTOPF recipes:

_____

_____

_____

_____

_____

_____

_____

_____

_____

_____

_____

_____

_____

For your own RÖMERTOPF recipes :

_____

_____

_____

_____

_____

_____

_____

_____

_____

_____

_____

_____

_____

_____

_____

For your own RÖMERTOPF recipes :

For your own RÖMERTOPF recipes:

_____

_____

_____

_____

_____

_____

_____

_____

_____

_____

_____

_____

_____

_____

For your own RÖMERTOPF recipes:

_____

_____

_____

_____

_____

_____

_____

_____

_____

_____

_____

_____

_____

_____

_____

For your own RÖMERTOPF recipes:

_____

_____

_____

_____

_____

_____

_____

_____

_____

_____

_____

_____

_____

_____

For your own RÖMERTOPF recipes :

_____

_____

_____

_____

_____

_____

_____

_____

_____

_____

_____

_____

_____

_____

_____

For your own RÖMERTOPF recipes :

_____

_____

_____

_____

_____

_____

_____

_____

_____

_____

_____

_____

_____

For your own RÖMERTOPF recipes :

_____

_____

_____

_____

_____

_____

_____

_____

_____

_____

_____

_____

_____

List of Main Recipes

THE FISH RÖMERTOPF, 77

VEGETABLES AND CEREALS, 93

Index